This work is published with assistance from the Liverpool Irish Festival and the Heritage Lottery Fund.

First published : October 2013

Published by: Liverpool Authors

Printed by : Twentyfourseven Design and Print

ISBN: 9780956452719

Front cover design: Moira Gil.

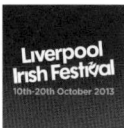

Liverpool
Irish Festival
10th-20th October 2013

A HIDDEN HISTORY

IRISH IN LIVERPOOL

An Ghaeilge i Learpholl

Tony Birtill

Dedication:

To my mother: Julia Daly (Síle Ní Dhálaigh) 1915-1977. Crois Ghearla, Co. na Mí, Éire.

Buíochas-Thanks

The Heritage Lottery Fund, the Liverpool Irish Festival and Cath Butterworth (Project manager, Finding the Liverpool Irish).

Greg Quiery who edited the final draft of this book and Professor Pádraig O Siadhail and Róis Máire Nic Giolla who read and advised on earlier drafts.

Professor Frank Neal (1932-2011) who gave me advice, shared information and recommended other sources of information to me.

Dr John Dunleavy who gave me advice and information.

Dr Peter Doyle, who generously translated MS APF Scritture Rif. Anglia Vol 10 pp 225ff and granted me permission to use the contents, which are copyright to him.

Dr Meg Whittle at Liverpool Metropolitan Cathedral Archive.

Greg Harkin at All Hallows College, Dublin, Archive

Howard Hague at the Unitarian Church Archive, London.

Brian Kirby, Capuchin Provincial Archives, Dublin.

Aaron Kiely and Peter Henegan at the Catholic Pictorial, Liverpool

Frank McIvor (1937-2013) for his advice and help with research on Merseyside.

Michael Kelly, author, Liverpool, for advice and sharing information with me.

Martin Collins, House of Commons, Westminster, for advice and sharing information with me.

Bernard Morgan, Liverpool, for advice.

Máirtín O Muilleoir and Michael Flanigan, Belfast for advice.

Staff at : Rawtenstall Central Library, Lancashire. Ormskirk Library, Lancashire. Sefton Libraries : Orrell, Bootle and Crosby (Local History Unit) Liverpool Libraries: Walton, Spellow and Central Library and Archive.

Hope University Library, Liverpool and Special Collections.

University of Liverpool Sydney Jones Library and Special Collections.

National Museum of Ireland, Dublin   National Library of Ireland.

Conradh na Gaeilge HQ Dublin.

St Michael's Irish Centre, Liverpool, for the use of their library, publishing advice/help , and Maureen and Patrick Morrison for their help with IT

Oideas Gael College, Glencolmcille, Co. Donegal, Ireland, for use of their library and bookshop and to the staff for IT assistance.

Seán Reid for IT assistance.

Walton on the Hill History Group

Linda Ervine, East Belfast Mission (Methodist)

I am bound to have overlooked somebody in this list- so thanks to whoever you may be!

To Liz and Liam for their patience as I researched and wrote this book

7

Contents

FORWARD
Dr Brian Stowell

An leabhar atá scríofa ag Tony Birtill maidir le stair na Gaeilge i Learpholl, nuair a bhí sé léite agam, thuig mé go bhfuil obair an-tábhachtach déanta aige, gan dabht. Is iontach go deo é go mbíonn duine acadúil ar bith ag rá fós go raibh formhór na nÉireannach bochta b'eigean dóibh teacht go Learpholl le linn an Ghorta Mhóir ina mBéarlóirí thar rud ar bith eile. Is soiléir ó leabhar Tony nach fíor é sin in aon chor. Agus cuireann a leabhar in iúl dúinn na polasaithe polaitiúla náireach a thug na hEireannaigh agus a dteanga faoi chois arís is arís eile. Ach cé go bhfuair na mílte bás, iad sin a bhí fágtha, d'fhan an misneach go láidir ina lán acu, agus chuaigh an misneach sin ó ghlúin go glúin go dtí an lá atá inniu ann. Bíonn cáilíochtaí speisialta ag muintir Learphoill, agus tháinig a lán de na cáilíochtaí sin ó mhuintir na hÉireann – bíonn misneach, cairdiúlacht is dánacht i measc na cáilíochtaí sin. Bhí sé de phribhléid agam a bheith ag obair i Learpholl le blianta fada agus buaileadh le daoine mar Tony Birtill. Is cóir go mbeidh a lán daoine ag léamh a leabhar éachtach, go háirithe daoine a thugann grá don Ghaeilge.

When I'd read the book written by Tony Birtill about the history of the Irish language in Liverpool, I appreciated that he'd carried out some very important work, without any doubt. It's remarkable that any academic is still asserting that the majority of the poor Irish people who were forced to come to Liverpool during the Great Famine were English speaking above all else. It's clear from Tony's book that this is not true at all. And his book describes for us the shameful political policies which trampled the Irish people and their language underfoot again and again. But although thousands died, courage remained strongly in many of those who were left, and that courage went down from generation to generation to the present day. The people of Liverpool have special qualities, and many of those qualities came from the people of Ireland – courage, friendliness and boldness are among those qualities. It was my privilege to be working in Liverpool for many years and to meet people like Tony Birtill. Many people should read his powerful book, especially those who love the Irish language.

Brian Stowell

Dúlais, Manainn – Douglas, Isle of Man

Lunasa 2013   Aug 2013

Dr Brian Stowell is a linguist, physicist and author. He isYn Lhaider (The reader) to Tynwald, the Parliament of the Isle of Man. He is fluent in Manx and Irish. He broadcasts regularly on Manx Radio. In 2008 he was awarded the Manx Heritage Foundation's *Reih Bleeaney Vanannan* (Manannan's Choice of the Year) award for outstanding contributions to Manx culture. On Tynwald Day 2010, he was awarded the Tynwald Honour, the highest honour that Tynwald can award a citizen. His publications include *Contoyryssyn Ealish ayns Cheer ny Yindyssyn*, a Manx translation of *Alice's Adventures in Wonderland*, and *Dunveryssyn yn Tooder-Folley (The Vampire Murders)*

Introduction

Some of the material in this book was originally published in Irish in the monthly internet magazine www.beo.ie. However, I realise that this is a minority language and so many people will be unaware of what I have written.

I particularly wanted the information to be available to the people of Liverpool, where I was born and grew up. As I researched this book I found that I was not the first person from Blessed Sacrament Parish, Walton, who was captivated by the Irish language and who was active in the Gaelic League. Stephen McKenna (1873-1934) who was born on Rice Lane, Walton, and who features in the last chapter of this book, was an early pioneer in this field and is clearly someone who should be recognised and celebrated in his home city. The same can be said for all the other talented, Liverpool-born Irish speakers who also feature in that chapter and who made such an outstanding contribution to the Gaelic Revival in the late nineteenth and early twentieth century.

I heard the Irish language when I was growing up; my mother - who had come to England to work as a nurse before the War - listened to ' Radio Athlone' as the state broadcaster was known They sometimes broadcast programmes and songs in Irish. On occasion my Aunt Greta - also a nurse - would visit. I remember them speaking Irish together. The Sunday Press published a cartoon in Irish called 'Flip' and I used to ask my mother to read it to me. When I discovered an Irish-English dictionary in Walton Library I noticed that a stamp inside indicated that it had been on long-term loan to Walton Prison. This made this mysterious language seem even more exciting to me! When I went to Cardinal Godfrey Technical School in Everton, aged 11 years, I heard the Irish Christian Brothers there speak Irish to each other. To my disappointment they did not teach it to us as it was not on the syllabus and quite frankly was not regarded as being of any value to someone growing up in England. The Liverpool Irish Centre on Mount Pleasant had a policy of putting up signs - such as 'Baill amháin' (members only) – in Irish, but that was about the only place in the city that did so (the exception being the Fenian monument in Ford Cemetery which carries the motto 'A Dhia, Saor Éire').

While studying Economic History and Economics at the University of East Anglia (1972-75) I found that our course books - such as Hobsbawm's Industry and Empire, Thompson's The Making of the English Working Class and Engel's The Condition of the Working Class in England - all dealt with the subject of the use of the Irish language amongst immigrants from that country, which came as no surprise to me.

It was only when I returned to live in Liverpool, after qualifying as a teacher at the University of London, that I went to Irish language night classes, taught by Manxman Brian Stowell. I sat the GCE Ordinary Level examination and then the Advanced level. I then did an Irish Language course for teachers at Oideas Gael College in Donegal and ended up teaching Irish night classes myself.

I had also joined the Gaelic League and resurrected the Liverpool branch of the organisation. I learnt something of the history of the Gaelic League in Liverpool from older members like Cáitlín Nic Cába (1905-1998) and Seán McNamara (1928-2012) who told me that his mother had known the great poet Piaras Béaslaí, who was born in Everton. I had always meant to write this history, and did include a lot of it in articles I wrote in Irish for Beo. As the older members of our community passed on, the memories and stories they got from their parents were in danger of being lost forever. Worse still, some published histories of the period contained alarming inaccuracies. I felt that this needed to be challenged.

When the Liverpool Irish Festival was awarded Heritage Lottery Funding for local studies in 2011 I volunteered to write a study on the use of the Irish language in Liverpool. It turned into this book.

Tony Birtill

June 2013

Notes on the author:

Tony Birtill was born in Walton, Liverpool . He attended Walton RC Primary School (Blessed Sacrament) and then Cardinal Godfrey High School in Everton with the Irish Christian Brothers. A graduate of the University of East Anglia (Economic History and Economics) and the University of London Institute of Education, he taught for many years in further and higher education. He now works as a writer and journalist and is a frequent contributor to Irish language radio and television and The Irish Post newspaper. He also writes a monthly feature article for www.beo.ie . He is a qualified Mountain Leader and works in this capacity for Oideas Gael in Co. Donegal, Ireland and also further afield.

A HIDDEN STORY.

THE IRISH LANGUAGE IN LIVERPOOL.

A plaque in Irish/Gaelic and English at Clarence Dock gates, Liverpool, explains that 1,300,000 Irish migrants, fleeing from the Great Hunger, arrived in Liverpool during the years 1845-1852. Even though many of these people subsequently moved on to other parts of England, or the USA and Canada, the arrival of such a vast number exerted a huge influence on a town with a population of around 300,000. One only has to look at the large number of Irish surnames in the current Liverpool telephone directory to appreciate the lasting impact the arrival of so many people has had. Frank Neal's two excellent books - 'Black '47, Britain and the Famine Irish ' and 'Sectarian Violence, the Liverpool Experience' - have gone some way to shed light on their tragic story.

As to the language they spoke, the conventional view is that there were few Irish speakers in Liverpool, and that the language had little impact on the culture of the city or the Irish community here. John Belchem, for example, in his introduction to his detailed study, 'Irish Catholic and Scouse' - makes the following reference: "In the absence of any phenotypic or linguistic difference (the overwhelming majority of the migrants being English-speakers)......"[1] In the pages below I will be challenging this viewpoint, bringing forward evidence to show that there were large numbers of Irish speakers in Liverpool throughout the nineteenth and early twentieth centuries, that they struggled to obtain the services of Irish speaking Catholic clergy, that there were both Catholic and Protestant Irish speakers in Liverpool, and that Liverpool played a significant part in the Irish language revival movement of the twentieth century. I will argue that the overwhelming majority of Irish migrants coming into Liverpool were mother-tongue (or first language) Irish speakers and English was their second language.

Another factor, frequently overlooked, is that the type of English spoken by these Irish migrants in itself constituted a linguistic difference : it was Hiberno-English, which consists of a mainly English vocabulary, interspersed with Gaelic words and often using Irish syntax. For example, in Irish : " An gob atá air !" which literally means ;" the beak on him !" is heard to this day in Liverpool as :" the gob on him !"; 'gob' ' being the Irish word for a beak but used as a slang word for ' mouth.' The use of the preposition 'air' meaning 'on him' is typical of Hiberno-English.

Assertions that the majority of migrants were English speakers, imply that there was a minority who were not. If there were monoglot Irish speakers arriving in England, they surely must have come from a society where the Gaelic language was very strong and widespread and where there were a lot of people whose first language was Irish but who could speak some English or were bilingual. As the Irish language had no official standing in Ireland and was discriminated against, there was considerable pressure on people to gain a knowledge of English in order to conduct business with state officials. To survive in England, the monoglot Irish speakers would have needed the help of those with a knowledge of English, and this comes across in the case studies provided below. Irish was a language spoken by millions of people throughout Ireland in the mid-nineteenth century, particularly west of a line from Derry in the north to Cork in the south. These were the very areas from which most famine refugees came in the period 1845-1852. I intend to show that a large proportion of these migrants were monoglot Irish speakers, many were bilingual and probably only a minority were monoglot English speakers, with no knowledge of Gaelic whatsoever.

I will also demonstrate that Irish speakers were held in very low regard by those with power over them, including government and its agencies, business people and the Catholic Church. Such attitudes made it more difficult for Irish speakers to escape from the cycle of poverty in which they were trapped, and was a

---

[1] Belchem, J. Irish, Catholic and Scouse.The history of the Liverpool Irish , 1800-1939. Liverpool U.P. 2007. P. 10

significant factor in accelerating the decline of their ancient language. The linguistic distinctiveness of the Irish, be it Gaelic, Hiberno-English or a mixture of both, was remarked on by contemporary observers, frequently with racist overtones. For example, the 1842 edition of The Picturesque Hand-book to Liverpool directed visitors to the Clarence Dock to observe the arrival of the Irish ferries :"At the stern will be seen, as usual, a freight of bipeds, old and young, holding converse in a jargon that it would be difficult to interpret; while the rest of the deck will be crowded with a medley of sheep, pigs and oxen." [2]

In all likelihood, the people would have been speaking Irish, one of the oldest vernaculars in Europe, with a literature that far pre-dated that of English. Note how the migrants are referred to as "bipeds" and not people, and that they are grouped with the animals. This accords with the view that sections of English society held towards the Irish, regarding them as some sort of sub-species, and as such not to be mourned when so many were exterminated during the period 1845-1852.[3] Similar sentiments were famously expressed in the magazine Punch : "A creature manifestly between the Gorilla and the Negro is to be met with in some of the lowest districts of London and Liverpool by adventurous explorers. It comes from Ireland, whence it has contrived to migrate; it belongs in fact to a tribe of Irish savages, the lowest species of Irish Yahoo. When conversing with its kind it talks a sort of gibberish," [4]

I believe that the question of what language these Irish migrants spoke is a vital one : not only does it help us to understand them as individuals, it also helps us to understand why they were treated the way they were by the British government and authorities. The establishment view was expressed by Lord Lyndhurst (1772-1863) during a debate on the Irish Municipal Reform Bill in February, 1837. Lyndhurst - who was three times Lord Chancellor - told his colleagues in Parliament : "It seems, my lords, that we Protestant Englishmen are to be governed by those who are aliens in blood, in language, in religion."[5]

He also attacked the Dissenters – Protestants outside the established Church -in his tirade, which was widely criticised both at the time and during and after the Famine. However, nobody complained about Lyndhurst's reference to the fact that Irish people spoke a different language, as this was manifestly true. The objections came mainly because Ireland, since the Act of Union of 1801, was part of the United Kingdom, and so Irish people could not be classed as 'aliens.' They were United Kingdom subjects with the same rights as every other subject, in theory at least. Pro-democracy campaigners of the day recognised that this did not apply in practice. Dublin Magazine, quoting Lyndhurst's comments on Ireland, pointed out that "....politically she is treated as 'alien in blood, language and religion.'"[6] It described Lord Lyndhurst's words as :"this never to be forgotten phrase."

Samuel Smiles (1812-1904) argued that Ireland was treated as a colony, in which the natives were "plundered." This is a reference to the huge exports of food which took place from the country to satisfy the expanding English economy. Many peasants grew potatoes to feed themselves and handed over any grain crops or animals they produced in order to pay their rent to the landlords, many of whom lived in England. Tithes to the established church – to which they did not belong - also had to be paid. This meant that they were always in danger of death by starvation when the potato crop failed , as it did in 1739-41, 1821, 1829 and 1830. Samuel Smiles noted that when Lord Lyndhurst made his statement about aliens in the House of Lords, it was " amidst ' hear, hears', and great applause."[7] The fact that the British establishment regarded the Irish as aliens helps to explain why they did so little as more than one million died in the most horrible circumstances in the period 1845-52 and more than one million others were forced into exile, an exile which took them first to the Clarence Dock, Liverpool.

Most of these people were intensely proud of their Gaelic culture. Some - from within the Irish community in Liverpool, including members of the second generation born in the city - went on to produce important works of literature in Irish or affirmed their love of the language through the arts. To claim that these people had no separate linguistic heritage is, I believe, both incorrect and an insult to their memory.

[2] Quoted in Belchem, op cit p 12

[3] See appendix 1 for discussion on 'extermination' in this context.

[4] Quoted in Curtis, L. Nothing But the Same Old Story, London 1984. P61, from Apes &Angels, Curtis, LP. London 1971 page 100

[5] Campbell, J & Campbell Hardcastle, M.S, Lives of Lord Lyndhurst and Lord Broughton . London 1869. Page 118. Quoted from Hansard

[6] The Dublin Magazine, Vol 1. 'Legislation in 1839. Page 128. (Free e book)

[7] Smiles, S. History of Ireland under the Government of England. London 1844. Page 53

WERE THERE SIGNIFICANT NUMBERS OF IRISH SPEAKERS IN LIVERPOOL?

Growing up in the North End of Liverpool, I was fascinated by the Irish language and went out of my way to learn to speak it fluently. However, the separate linguistic and cultural heritage of the Irish community in Britain is no secret : the prominent English historian EP Thompson comments on it , describing :"The enormously rich inheritance of Irish song and folklore," of the immigrants.[8] Although he argues that the Gaelic language and culture did not usually survive into the second generation (something I will challenge in this book) at least he recognises that they had a separate language and culture when they arrived in England.

Similarly, EJ Hobsbawn comments on the strength of the distinctive culture of the Irish immigrants, and although he argues that some had a "knowledge of English," others were Irish speaking. [9]

The Irish presence in Liverpool goes back a long way. King John granted the town recognition as a borough in 1207 in order to use it as a port to invade Ireland. The links between Liverpool and Ireland have continued ever since; for example, it was noted in the 1590's that Irish and other foreign merchants who lodged in the seaport had refused to attend chapel on Sundays. [10]A large number of Irish Protestants arrived in the town in the 1640s in order to escape the violence of the rebellion there (see later section on Bedell) while an even larger number arrived during the rising of 1798.[11]

The greatest wave of migrants from Ireland arrived during the Famine, 1845-1852. However, as the table below shows, there was already a long-established Irish community in the city, comprising 17.3% of the population in 1841.

Irish-born residents in the borough of Liverpool

Year	1841	1851	1861	1871	1891
Population	286,656	375,955	443,938	493,405	517,980
Number of Irish born	49,639	83,813	83,949	76,761	66,071
Irish born as % of pop	17.3	22.3	18.9	15.5	12.6

(From : F. Neal : Sectarian Violence . The Liverpool experience)

100 years before this, St Mary's Catholic Chapel in Lumber Street, off Old Hall Street, began a baptismal register, which shows a "striking predominance of Irish surnames and several places of residence given as 'of' or 'formerly from' Ireland." [12] This demonstrates that there was significant migration from Ireland around 1741, well before the arrival of famine refugees in the 19th century. This church was completely destroyed by a loyalist mob on April 30, 1746, angry at the 1745 Rising in Scotland. The Catholics built another, disguised as a warehouse, in Edmund Street, but this too was destroyed by a mob in 1759, and was subsequently rebuilt. The Benevolent Society of St Patrick had been set up in the city in 1807, with the sole aim "the educating and apprenticing of Irish children of all denominations ." [13] The school they founded still stands in Pleasant Street, off Clarence Street.

The foundation stone for St Patrick's Church, Park Place, in the South End, was laid on March 17 1821 while St Anthony's on Scotland Road in the North End was completed in 1833. Both these churches catered mainly for Irish-speaking Catholics and it is clear that strong contacts were maintained with the Catholic Church in Ireland. However, the build-up to the opening of St Patrick's in 1827 was marred by controversy as it was rumoured that an English priest was to be appointed to the new church. This would have meant that hundreds of Irish parishioners, who had little or no English, would have been unable to attend confession, as they are required to do by their church. In the end, Irishman Francis Murphy (1795-1858) from County Meath was appointed to the role. This aided fund raising for the new building and avoided conflict with the English Catholic hierarchy.

[8] Thompson, EP. The Making of the English Working Class . Penguin 1968. P 480

[9] Hobsbawm, EJ. Industry and Empire. Pelican 1969. P. 310

[10] Hollinshead,JE. Liverpool in the 16th Century. Lancaster 2007. P 147

[11] Brooke, R. Liverpool as it Was 1775-1800. First pub: 1853. New edition, Liverpool 2003. P300-301

[12] Ascott, Lewis and Power. Liverpool 1660-1750. Liverpool UP 2006. P 55

[13] Burke, T. Catholic History of Liverpool. Liverpool 1910. Page 32

In 1836 John McHale - Archbishop of Tuam, County Galway from 1834-1881 - paid a visit to Liverpool and preached at St Patrick's Church. "His arrival was signalised by great rejoicing on the part of the Irish population, and the sum of two hundred pounds was placed in the offertory bags at the morning service towards reducing the debt on the Church."[14] John McHale was a great supporter of the Irish language and published an Irish translation of the New Testament in 1846, followed by translations of other parts of the scriptures. "That these books ran into at least two editions proves that there was a demand for bibles among Irish Catholics."[15]

THE CATHOLIC CHURCH AND THE IRISH LANGUAGE

How did Irish speakers cope with life in the English speaking environment of Liverpool? Learning English was the obvious course, especially amongst the second generation. In the core streets where the Irish community dominated, there would have been many situations in which people could operate through the medium if Irish, including on family occasions and when using local services such as markets and shops. In dealings with municipal officials and other aspects of the state, Irish speakers had to utilise English, probably with the assistance of a friend or relative who could speak the language to the required standard. Many of the professionals, tradesmen and business people – such as shop keepers – working in the Irish community were themselves Irish and would have been able to speak the Irish language if required. The Bligh brothers, both doctors, are good examples. For most Irish Catholics at this time, it was the Church above all else which was the most significant agency in their everyday life, whether for daily and weekly worship, ceremony on significant occasions such as marriage, or for health and welfare support for the poor. How did the Church respond to the needs of Irish speakers in their congregations?

Although Lancashire had the largest and strongest native English Catholic population in the country, in the eighteenth century Liverpool was predominantly Protestant and it is clear that the city's Catholics were mainly Irish immigrants. Although the Lancashire Catholic hierarchy were happy to see the numerical increase in church membership brought about by the Irish Catholic immigrants, it was clear early on that they wished to maintain their English identity and that they were not going to cater especially for the Irish newcomers. "A small indication of this was the very few churches dedicated to Irish saints throughout the diocese."[16]

The diocese of Liverpool was created in September 1850 when Pope Pius IX re-established the Catholic hierarchy in Britain and Ireland; prior to that England was classed as a missionary country and together with Wales came under the Roman Congregation for the Propagation of the Faith , which was known as Propaganda. England and Wales were divided into districts and the Lancashire District was, from 1836, under the control of the Vicar Apostolic George Brown (1786-1856) who was from Fylde in Lancashire. He became the first Bishop of the new Liverpool diocese in 1850. He appears to have been particularly anti-Irish : in 1841 he confided to his colleague Vicar Apostolic John Briggs that he was finding it very difficult to find enough priests, but did not wish to recruit more Irishmen in this role.[17] This is rather ironic, given that it was an Irish saint, Aidan, who brought Christianity to the north of England in 635 AD.

Priests from mainland Europe appear to have had a better understanding of the crucial role of the Irish in the history of the church and as such were generally more sympathetic towards them. Fr Luigi Gentili, the Rosminian missioner who was entrusted by Propaganda with the task of reporting on the state of English Catholicism, complained to Rome in 1841 about the attitude of Brown and his like towards the Irish, saying that many of the Irish in England were 'abandoned for want of pastors who never put their foot in the areas where they live and so they miserably perish' .[18] Gentili, a multi-linguist, spent nearly two years (1829 – 30) living and studying in the Irish College in Rome, where he became familiar with the Irish language as well as improving his English. He made a point of visiting the Irish communities in England, including that in Liverpool. He conducted a mission in Ireland at the height of the famine and died of typhoid, caught while hearing the confessions of the poor, in Dublin in 1848.

Matters came to a head in Liverpool in 1842 when 24,000 Irish Catholics (representing nearly half of the Irish-born residents of the city) signed a petition to Propaganda in Rome, organised by a local Irish

---

[14] Burke, T. Catholic History of Liverpool. P.54

[15] Moffit, M. The Society for Irish Church Missions to the Roman Catholics 1849-1950. Manchester UP 2010. Page 22

[16] Doyle, P. Mitres and Missions in Lancashire. Bluecoat, Liverpool 2005. P47

[17] Doyle, P. Mitres and Missions in Lancashire. Liverpool 2005. P 77

[18] Doyle, P. Mitres and Missions in Lancashire. Liverpool 2005. Pp 40-41

society, led by cattle salesman Charles Leonard, publican John 'Jack' Langan and customs officer Edmund Griffin. The petition claimed that very little was being done to help the Irish spiritually and that some English Catholics were even putting obstacles in the way of the few Irish priests who tried to help. "The main lack, the petitioners claimed, was of priests who could speak Gaelic, so that large numbers could not go to confession; even the mission of St Patrick's, built specifically for the Irish, had no Irish priest."[19] Fr Francis Murphy had left St Patrick's for Australia in 1838 (he subsequently became the first Bishop of Adelaide) and the petitioners claimed that he had suffered "persecution" at the hands of aristocratic English Catholics. They also cited Dr Thomas Butler, a curate at St Anthony's, as another Irish priest who had been badly treated. The parish priest at St Anthony's (1825-1844), Peter Wilcock, was English.

George Brown had declined to renew Dr Butler's faculties "because of rumours of unsavoury conduct." The row rumbled on until the following year, when Propaganda , while refusing to re-appoint Dr Butler, promised to do whatever it could to promote the faith among the Irish in Liverpool. Brown's reluctance to appoint Irish priests was subsequently overtaken by events, as ten of his clergymen (mainly English) died while attending to the victims of 'famine fever' in 1847. He was forced to appeal to seminaries in Ireland for replacements. (see next chapter)

The Vatican was well-informed about the controversy surrounding the lack of Irish-speaking clergy in Liverpool. In May 1843, Thomas Cullen wrote to his brother, Father Paul Cullen in Rome telling him that the dispute which had given rise to the massive petition was over.[20]Thomas and another brother, Garrett, together with their brother in law Thomas Verdon, ran the Liverpool firm Cullen and Verdon which dominated the lucrative Anglo-Irish cattle trade. The Cullens were from a prosperous Kildare farming family and Paul (1803- 1878) lived in Rome for 30 years. He was consecrated Archbishop of Armagh and Primate of All Ireland, in Rome, in February 1850. He had been appointed Rector of the Irish College in Rome in 1832 and as such he fulfilled the function of the Irish hierarchy's official agent in the Vatican. (see later section on Irish colleges) His brothers, nephews and sister in Liverpool were very well-informed about matters on both sides of the Irish Sea and wrote to him nearly every month appraising him of developments, so that he had a first-hand, non-clerical take on events. He also stayed with members of the family in Liverpool and so was personally familiar with events and issues in the city.

Further evidence of the importance of the Irish language in Liverpool was provided by the visit of Fr Theobald Mathew (1790-1856) in July 1843 when he administered the temperance pledge in both Irish and English at a number of venues, including St Patrick's and St Anthony's. "The tide of emigration flowed rather steadily in those days towards certain English centres, and hence the necessity of using the Irish form which was as follows :"Geallaim le cabhair Dé, gan aon sórt ólacháin mheisceamhail a dhéanamh aris go bráth." (I promise, with God's help, to abstain forever from any sort of alcoholic drink)[21]

Around 70,000 people took the pledge in Liverpool, to the extent that a number of public houses closed down or, in the case of John McArdle in the strongly Irish-speaking area of Crosbie Street, changed use for a time to become a part- grocery store.[22] Fr Mathew spent three months in England. In addition to Liverpool he visited cities such as Manchester and London. He is estimated to have administered the pledge to 600,000 people in that time.

Fr Mathew returned to Liverpool during the Famine in 1849, and again in 1854 when he called at the home of Fr James Nugent (1822-1905). Nugent had been a student in Rome when Fr Mathew had made his earlier 'triumphant' tour and so this was their first meeting. He impressed upon Nugent that the temperance campaign was about more than condemning the use of alcohol. We see elements of this philosophy when Nugent founded the Total Abstinence League of the Cross in Liverpool in 1872 (following a tour in America). [23]The League of the Cross Hall which he built in 1875 was to become an important social and cultural centre for the Irish community in the city, where those who spoke Irish felt at home.

Despite the hostility of some Lancashire Catholic leaders to the increasing Irish influence in the county,

[19] Ibid. P 41

[20] Papers of Paul Cullen 799. 25/5/1843. www.irishcollege.org

[21] Hayden, A. Footprints of Father Mathew. Dublin 1947 . p 286

[22] Denvir, J. Life Story of an Old Rebel. Dublin 1910. P 16

[23] Furnival, J. Children of the Second Spring. Gracewing 2005. Pp 202-203

and especially in Liverpool, Archbishop John McHale returned to preach in the city in 1851. He was accompanied by Archbishop Cullen. He preached at St Nicholas' in support of the Catholic schools in the city, the establishment of which was seen as crucial for maintaining the faith amongst the young.[24] We have accurate statistics for the size of the Irish community in Vauxhall (St Anthony's parish) in 1842 from a survey conducted there that year by Finch.[25] By far the largest group of heads of households amongst "the labouring classes" in Vauxhall were born in Ireland , followed by those born in Liverpool (though many of these would also have been of Irish origin). Lancashire and lastly Wales followed in descending order. Finch mentions that a local school – North Corporation - conducted along the lines of an Irish National School, had been "eminently successful" until the newly elected Tory city council insisted that the school reverted to using only Anglican worship, with the result that Catholic and Dissenter pupils left. The roll dropped from 875 in 1841 to 301 in 1851.

In the National Schools in Ireland, children of all denominations were taught together. However, all lessons were taught in English, so Irish children would have to learn that language first. Their own language was not on the curriculum! Presumably this was also the case in the school in Liverpool. The controversy around the 'Anglican take over' of the Liverpool Corporation schools led Fr. Francis Murphy, senior priest at St Patrick's, to write to Dublin in 1837 to arrange for the Irish Christian Brothers to come to Liverpool to set up a school next to his church in Park Place. Edmund Rice (1762-1844), who had founded the order in Kilkenny to educate the poor, arranged this personally. The school was a great success and by 1845 the Brothers were running six schools in the city, including St Anthony's on Scotland Road and Copperas Hill School (St Nicholas').[26]

The Christian Brothers were great champions of the Irish language- their Irish Grammar Book became a standard textbook throughout Irish schools in the 20th century. They were obviously sensitive to the cultural background of the children in their schools in Liverpool : John Denvir states that he was taught nothing about Ireland at Copperas Hill School until the Christian Brothers came. "I shall always be grateful to that noble body of men, not only for their religious but for the national training they gave." He describes how they gave the pupils a map of Ireland and taught them the correct Irish pronunciation of the place names.[27] Presumably, the lessons were conducted in the English language, but the brothers would have been able to converse in Irish with children who spoke that language and perhaps even taught them to read and write in it. It is well known that Edmund Rice insisted that the Irish Christian Brothers were to be solely responsible for the internal management of the schools "without any control on the part of the priests or the committee."[28] Perhaps he was aware of the Anglo-centric outlook on the part of the hierarchy in Lancashire.

It was one of the Irish Christian Brothers at St Patrick's, Br Joseph Maher, who established the St Patrick's Guild in Liverpool in1842. Modelled on the St Patrick's Society in which the Brothers in London were involved, its aim was ensure that its members kept to their religious duties (including confession and holy communion.) It also acted as friendly society, providing help in the event of sickness or death. It had enrolled 366 young men by 1844. Its members were prominent in the campaign for more Irish-speaking priests to be recruited to Liverpool

THE STANDING OF IRISH AMONGST CATHOLIC CLERGY.

There was a shortage of Catholic priests generally in England and Ireland, especially Irish speaking clergy, after the foundation of Maynooth College in 1795. The Penal Laws had meant that Catholic priests were trained in mainland Europe at 'Irish' Colleges mainly located in university towns such as Louven (Belgium) ,Paris, Lille, Lisbon, Prague and Salamanca. There were two such colleges in Rome : St Isadores (founded by the Irish Franciscan Luke Wadding in 1618) and the Irish College (founded in 1628), run by Jesuits and secular priests. As Irish was the language of the majority of Irish people up to the mid-nineteenth century, it was the language that was used in the Irish colleges in Europe. Many Irish priests were remarkable linguists and would be competent in Latin, French, Spanish and English as well as their own language. The Irish colleges were held in great esteem in Europe,(where the Irish role in

[24] Burke, T. Catholic History of Liverpool 1910. P 98

[25] Finch, J. Statistics of the Vauxhall Ward, 1842. Facsimile edition, Liverpool 1986

[26] Gillespie, W. The Christian Brothers in England, 1825-1880. Bristol 1975. P 68

[27] Denvir, J. Life Story of an Old Rebel. P 14

[28] Gillespie, W. Christian Brothers in England 1825-1880. P 68

spreading Christianity in the sixth century was renowned) and many clerics and scholars from other countries learnt the Irish language in them. One institution records that "The first endowment for the teaching of Irish in modern times was set up in the college (Paris)".[29] The Irish colleges in Rome, Paris and Louven all developed fonts for printing Irish books, Irish catechisms and works of piety, which were produced to assist priests when they returned home. In 1768 Bishop John O' Brien of Cloyne published an Irish dictionary in Paris. Nobody could have conceived that one of the most ancient and learned languages in Europe would go into such catastrophic decline in the late nineteenth century.

Irish had no official standing under British rule and so English made continuous headway. In 1773 Archbishop John Carpenter of Dublin, himself an Irish scholar, informed the Pope that the bishops of Ireland believed it essential that the students at the Irish College in Rome be trained in both Irish and English. When the French revolutionaries suppressed the Paris Irish College in 1792 the Irish bishops petitioned the British Government for permission to establish a seminary in Ireland. When France declared war on England in February 1793 the situation looked more promising for the Irish hierarchy. The Catholic Relief Act of April 1793 allowed Catholics to take degrees at Trinity College, Dublin. St Patrick's College, Carlow, was opened later that year as the first institution of higher education for Catholics. The seminary at Maynooth was established in 1795. As this was a government -funded institution, it was English-speaking . Roy Foster goes further, arguing: " the theory was that an Anglicized Catholic church would evolve if priests were not trained in Europe, and were not drawn from the Irish-speaking peasantry."[30] He argues that the Maynooth priests came to represent the families of strong farmers and shopkeepers rather than the Irish-speaking cottier class. However, given the strength of the language amongst the peasantry, the Catholic merchants and large farmers would have needed a working knowledge of the language in order to communicate with those to whom they wished to sell products or hire on their farms. This was certainly the case with the uncles of Daniel O' Connell (1775-1847)[31]

There were some Irish classes at Maynooth : Paul O' Brien, a native speaker of the language from County Meath and a popular poet and scholar, was employed as an Irish teacher while a student at the college in 1804. He was later made Professor of Irish after a man named Keenan from Dublin left money in his will to endow a chair of Irish[32] . Although French was the language of the professors' table, O' Brien apparently organised a corner where the language was Irish "He continually pleaded the cause of the language with the church authorities and would seem to have been one of the first to argue that the language would act as a buffer against irreligion and materialism." [33] The Practical Grammar of the Irish Language by Paul O Brien was published by Maynooth in 1809. He was clearly an inspiration to his students as two of them published Irish works shortly after his early death in 1820.

Significantly, a letter from C.W. Russell, Maynooth, to Paul Cullen in Rome in 1847 makes reference to a number of Irish language texts. Cullen had received an Irish Grammar the year before from Cork.[34] However, O Céirin argues that the decade before the famine seems to have been one of neglect of Irish at Maynooth. James Tully, who was professor of Irish from 1828-1876 was apparently a reluctant appointee to the position : "The professor was uninspiring and the language regarded as doomed."[35]

We have a first -hand account of the situation on the ground from John O'Donovan when he was working with the Ordnance Survey team in 1834. He asked the Rev. McArdle, a parish priest in Co. Down if the priests in general could speak Irish . "He said they could, but as they were all young dandies from Maynooth, they would not wish to let anyone know that they understood a word of it. 'Though,' he says with a sneer, 'they never heard a word of English from their grandmothers, nor probably from any one until they were 12 years of age.'"[36]

[29] O Cuív, B (ed) A View of the Irish Language. Dublin 1969. P 84 (Wall, M). 82-84

[30] Foster, R (ed) Illustrated History of Ireland. Oxford 1989. P 177

[31] MacDonagh, O. O'Connell. London 1991. P 8

[32] Corish, PJ. Maynooth College 1795-1995. Dublin 1995. P 52

[33] O Céirin, C. Translation of My Story by Peter O Leary. Cork1970. Appendix xi

[34] Letters of Paul Cullen 1401. 1/6/47. www.irishcollege.org

[35] Corish, PJ. Maynooth College 1795-1995 P 116

[36] Boyne, P. John O Donovan. Kilkenny 1987. P 27

Thus priests who were unwilling or unable to speak Irish often went to minister in Irish-speaking districts. This had important consequences which the Catholic Church was to regret. Firstly, it discouraged people from practising their religion through formal church structures- as noted above. Irish speakers could not attend confession and this meant that they could not then attend holy communion at mass, an essential component in Catholic worship. Also, visits to the sick, weddings, baptisms, funerals and so forth would be through a language the people might not understand and even dislike as they associated it with oppressive landlords and government officials. "In parts of rural Ireland, however, and especially in the areas where Gaelic was still spoken, there was, perhaps, a level of practice as low as 20-40%, with a lack of clear instruction in the Faith and little attention paid to the sacraments other than baptism and extreme unction." [37]

Secondly, this left the way open for Irish-speaking Protestant evangelists to spread their faith to the native population. Such evangelists were active in Liverpool, as well as in Ireland itself, particularly during the Famine. (See later section on the work of the IS and ICM.)

The lack of participation by Irish-speaking people in formal religious practice (or reading the Bible) did not mean that they were not religious. Religion was bound up in people's lives, and formed a crucial part of their individual, family and national identity. There were rituals at holy wells, pilgrimages, prayers and devotions - especially the Rosary – both at home and outdoors, all being part of what is now rather fashionably described as 'Celtic spirituality.' Certainly Peadar O' Laoghaire, who attended Maynooth 1861-1867, found saying the Rosary on his own in Irish, "like we used to do at home and north at Derrynamona while I was there," [38] was an antidote to the Anglo atmosphere he found in the college while training for the priesthood.

There was a certain amount of opposition to the imposition of English-speaking Catholic clergy : for example in 1798 the clergy of Kerry succeeded in preventing a Corkman from becoming bishop of the diocese, using the fact that he knew no Irish as one of the strongest arguments in their petition to the Pope. In 1856 Bishop Moriarty of Kerry spoke openly about his attachment to the Irish language while preaching at the funeral of his own predecessor, Corneilius Egan, in Killarney. [39] Seminaries established in places like Carlow, Kilkenny, Thurles, Waterford and Wexford appear to have been more sympathetic to the Irish language.

THE IRISH LANGUAGE AMONGST PROTESTANTS

While Irish speakers were predominantly Catholic in religion, there were substantial numbers of Irish speaking Protestants throughout the country, a fact of which Lord Lyndhurst appeared unaware. Some Irish-speaking Catholics converted to Protestantism in order to escape the persecution of the Penal Laws, especially with regard to the inheritance of property. Sometimes one family member would be nominated to do this. One well known example was Hugh Falvey, a conforming uncle of Daniel O'Connell, who saved much of the property of his Catholic relatives " on several occasions by fictitious or collusive legal actions." [40]

Some Irish-speaking Catholics converted because they favoured the Protestant version of Christianity ; for example Muircheartach O Cionga (1562-1639) from an Irish bardic family in Co. Offaly was converted and ordained in the established Anglican Church of Ireland in 1633. His translation of the Bible for Bedell [41] is referred to later.

The writer William Carleton (1794-1869) from Co. Tyrone, whose book Traits and Stories of the Irish Peasantry drew the attention of the Victorians to the separate linguistic heritage of the Irish people, considered becoming a Catholic priest before eventually converting to Protestantism. Some Irish-speakers switched back and forth between religions. For example John O'Daly (1800-1878) the Waterford-born author of the popular book Self Instruction in Irish, taught Irish at a Wesleyan School in Kilkenny. He later returned to Catholicism and ran his famous publishers and book store in Anglesea Street, Dublin. He was friends with all the major Irish writers and scholars of the time, including John

[37] Doyle, P. Mitres & Missions p 45

[38] O Céirin, C. My Story, Peter O Leary, trans. P 73. Cork 1970

[39] O Cuiv. A View of the Irish Language. Dublin 1969. P 84

[40] MacDonagh, O. O Connell. London 1991. P 5

[41] O Snodaigh, P. Hidden Ulster. Dublin 1977. P 11

O'Donovan.[42]

That there must have been substantial numbers of Irish-speaking Protestants can also be deduced by the large number of Protestants with Irish Gaelic surnames. For example, the present-day Unionist politician Dr Christopher McGimpsey, described Irish as :"..a language which our family lost some three hundred years ago," when he explained why he was learning it and pointed to fellow Unionist politicians like Ken Maginnis and Harold McCusker who also carried native Irish names .[43]

Irish -speaking agnostics, atheists and free-thinkers must also be included in the equation ; for example philosopher John Toland (1670-1722). He was born into an Irish-speaking Catholic family in Donegal, converted to Presbyterianism, but later became the foremost critic of religious orthodoxy of the period. His book 'Christianity not Mysterious', 1696, was banned by order of the Irish Parliament. He himself was forced to flee abroad. He lived in London from 1700 to1722.[44]

Scottish Gaelic speakers were among the Protestant settlers who came to Ulster in the 17th century. Other Protestants living in predominantly Irish-speaking areas throughout Ireland also learned the language :

"The dissenting minister of this place, Moses Neilson, is a most agreeable character, and a man of much culture and learning. He is perfection in Latin, Greek and Hebrew, as in the native Irish tongue. The Dissenters and Papists of this parish mostly speak in that language..." (Hugh Johnston, landlord of Rademon, near Crossgar, Co. Down, 1784)[45]

In the early 19th century, Ulster Presbyterians led the movement to promote the language. Irish was a part of the curriculum in the two most prestigious schools in Belfast- the Belfast Academy and the Belfast Academical Institution (BAI - founded in 1810.) "Both institutions had as headmasters Presbyterian ministers, the Rev, J Bryce and the Rev. William Neilson. Both were prominent in the Irish language movement in Belfast."[46] Irish was taught in the Belfast (later Royal) Academy as far back as the 1780s and in the Belfast (later Royal) Academical Institution during two periods in the 19th century. Neilson, from Co.Down - in his capacity as Professor of Irish at BAI - published a textbook : An Introduction to the Irish Language. "Much more important, perhaps, is the fact that there are several references to him preaching in Irish in Belfast itself and around the province, to Presbyterian congregations."[47]

Another group of Presbyterians, led by Robert MacAdam and R.J. Bryce, founded the Ulster Gaelic Society in 1828, along with Dr James McDonnell, a member of the Church of Ireland. Unlike some of the purely scholarly societies of the time, which aimed at the preservation of ancient manuscripts, the Ulster Gaelic Society had amongst its aims the maintenance of 'teachers of the Irish language where it most prevails ' and the publication of useful works in that tongue; that is to say, it was interested in Irish as a contemporary language."[48] Dr James MacDonnell (1763-1845) was a fluent Irish speaker, something which was obviously a useful asset for a medical practitioner when many patients were Irish speakers. (Dr John Bligh in Liverpool was another who found the Irish language an important professional asset). McDonnell helped to organise the famous Belfast Harp Assembly in 1792, the year the pro-democracy paper The Northern Star was founded in the city. That paper went on to publish the bilingual 'Gaelic Magazine' or ' Bolg an Tsolair ' in 1795 .

Robert McAdam, owner of the largest iron foundry in Belfast, also launched the Ulster Journal of Archaeology in 1853. He continued to edit and finance it until 1862. One of its aims was to promote and foster interest in the Irish language. It received a number of contributions from the Liverpool-based, Ulster-born Anglican clergyman Abraham Hume, who was both a keen historian and Irish-language enthusiast. Hume had learned to speak Irish in Liverpool.

John O'Donovan comments on the cordial relations which existed between the Protestant and Catholic clergymen he encountered while working on the Ordnance Survey in County Down. For example, he met

---

[42] Boyne, P. John O Donovan. 57

[43] Mistéil (ed) The Irish Language and the Unionist Tradition. Belfast 1994. McGimpsey p7

[44] Connolly, SJ. Oxford Companion to Irish History. OUP 1998.

[45] Ultach/Foras na Gaeilge : An Ghaeilge . Belfast 2012 .p 14

[46] O Buachalla, B. The Irish Language and the Unionist Tradition. Belfast 1994 . p 40

[47] Ibid. p 41

[48] O Buachalla, B. in The Irish Language and the Unionist Tradition. P 41

Rev McArdle (mentioned earlier) in the house of a Presbyterian clergyman.[49] When he visited the home of Rev Waring, the Church of Ireland Rector of Waringstown, Co. Down, the minister proceeded to examine him to find if he was really skilled in the Irish language ! Moffitt also notes the friendly relations which existed between Church of Ireland clergymen and the Catholic clergy, and Catholic community generally. This is one reason why many of them opposed the proselytising of the ICM.[50]

The Anglicans were early pioneers in using Irish to promote their faith. The Irish New Testament, which appeared in 1602, was translated by various clergymen, including Nicholas Walsh. The Book of Common Prayer followed in 1608. William Bedell (1571-1642) the Essex-born Bishop of Kilmore , Co. Cavan (1629-1642) encouraged divinity students to learn Irish when he was Provost of Trinity College Dublin in 1627. He commissioned the translation of the Old Testament into Irish, which was published posthumously in 1685. The Anglicans also founded the Irish Society (IS) in Dublin in 1818 "for promoting the education of the native Irish through the medium of their own language" and intended to "afford the same advantages for education to all classes of professing Christians."[51] Significantly, this organisation had a branch in Liverpool, as did the more hard-line Society for Irish Church Missions (ICM) which was founded in 1849 by the Church of England clergyman Revd. Alexander Dallas and which utilised the extreme hardship during Famine times to entice the starving to Protestantism.

Rev, James Henthorn Todd (1805-1869) continued the tradition of Bedell by co-founding St Columba's College, Rathfarnham, Dublin, in 1843. This school promoted the Irish language for those training for the Church of Ireland priesthood. One of its stated aims was :" to enable the Gospel to be preached in the Irish language.".[52] (See later reference to Coslett Ó Cuinn (1907-1995))

The Hibernian Bible Society (originally the Dublin Bible Society) was founded in Dublin in 1806 by Rev BW Mathias (1772-1841), a member of the evangelical wing of the Church of Ireland. It published and distributed bibles in both Irish and English. A Ladies Auxiliary Bible Society was founded in 1812. A central aim of Evangelists of course is to make the Bible available to everyone in their own language. This was often interpreted by Catholic leaders as proselytising, leading them to question the motives of colleges like St Columba's. However, the College's commitment to the Irish language was illustrated when its directors agreed to sponsor the production of the first modern Irish Grammar. The author, John O Donovan (1806-1861) had been searching for financial support for this project since 1828, without success. "The Directors of the College agreed to be responsible for the production of the Grammar, to use it in their senior classes and to give the author £100 for his work. The Grammar of the Irish Language was published in 1845."[53]O'Donovan dedicated the work to Rev. J.H. Todd and significantly, a copy was dispatched to Fr Paul Cullen, Rector of the Irish College in Rome, the following year by the Vincentians in Cork.[54] This would suggest that the Catholic Church was using the Grammar to train its own priests and was appreciative of the work carried out by the Church of Ireland for the Irish language. Maynooth College, the primary agency for the training of Catholic clergy in Ireland, did not participate in the Grammar project. The Practical Grammar produced by Paul O'Brien at Maynooth in 1809 was a much more modest volume.

Rev Todd, who was appointed librarian of Trinity College in 1852, worked alongside John O Donovan and Eugene O Curry (both Catholics) to classify and arrange the college's collection of Irish manuscripts. He spent a lot of money buying more manuscripts and rare books and obtained a record of Irish manuscripts in foreign libraries. He also edited the Irish version of a number of books himself. In 1835, the Presbyterian General Assembly passed a motion requiring Irish (which in 1841 it referred to as "our sweet and memorable mother tongue") to be studied by candidates for the ministry.[55] Given the above facts, it is no surprise that a survey conducted in 1850 by the Anglican Rev Abraham Hume in the districts of Vauxhall/St Stephens in Liverpool revealed a small but significant proportion of Irish speaking Protestant residents, some of whom appear to have been monoglots, demonstrating that – contrary to the

[49] Boyne, P. John O Donovan . Kilkenny 1987. P 27-28

[50] Moffitt, M. The ICM. MUP 2010 .pp 288-289

[51] Moffitt p 29

[52] Boyne, P. P 58

[53] Boyne, P. P 58

[54] Papers of Paul Cullen 1273. 10/11/1845. www.irishcollege.org

[55] Ultach/Foras na Gaeilge. An Ghaeilge. Belfast 2012. P 13

impression given by some historians - Irish Protestants were not all English-speakers.[56] Abraham Hume was one of a number of Irish Protestant clergymen who, although based in Britain, made a significant contribution to the preservation and revival of the Irish language.

Given the distinct cultural, and often linguistic differences of the Irish Presbyterians, it is not surprising that they established the Irish Islington Church in Liverpool in 1843 (Islington being, at that time, on the outskirts of Liverpool city centre). However the leaders of the Lancashire Presbyterians seemed no more inclined to tolerate the separate culture of their Irish brethren than the leaders of the Catholic Church in the county. A bitter dispute arose between the Liverpool Irish Presbyterians and the Presbytery of Lancaster which was only resolved when the name 'Irish ' was removed from the Islington chapel and the General Assembly of the Presbyterian Church in Ireland in 1850 disclaimed 'any intention of invading the jurisdiction or territory of the English Synod.' [57]

A similar situation arose with the Reformed Presbyterian Congregation in Liverpool - part of the Eastern Synod of the Reformed Presbyterian Church in Ireland - which tried to maintain links with Belfast in 1857, but was forced to link up with Glasgow instead. However, they continued to assist Ulster Presbyterian migrants passing through Liverpool en route to America.

Through its Home Mission the General Assembly of the Presbyterian Church of Ireland attempted to convert the Catholic population. To this end it set up stations in such strongly Irish speaking areas as Kerry and Connacht. Money for this work was collected in England and Scotland. With the heavy Irish emigration of the 1830s and 1840s, missions were also established in Britain. In 1842, the Home Missions announced the formation of a Ladies Association in Glasgow, which "like its sister in Edinburgh......takes a special interest in the instruction of the native Irish, through the medium of their own language." [58]George Field, an agent for the Home Mission living in Scotland wrote an Irish Grammar /text book for use by the organisation. The Grammar was published in Belfast in 1841.[59]

When the Gaelic League (Conradh na Gaeilge) was established in 1893 one of its first northern branches was in the largely Protestant Shankill Road area, Belfast, where 106 people in the 1911 census recorded themselves as Irish speakers. Other largely Protestant areas of Belfast also had their quota of Irish speakers, including Smithfield (547), Ormeau (529), Windsor (302) and St George (98). The curate of St George's parish was the Rev. Canon Feardocha Ó Conaill- a native Irish speaker and Rector's son- who was also lecturer in Irish at Queens University, Belfast(a post which was not filled for 40 years after John O Donovan died in 1862). [60]

The 1911 census showed there were around 8,000 Irish speakers in Belfast. Included in the East Belfast contingent were the Ervine family of Frome Street, who said on their census form that they could speak and write Irish as well as English. [61]These were fore-bears of the loyalist politician David Ervine (1953-2007), one of the founders of the Popular Unionist Party. The current generation of Ervines have renewed the family interest in the Irish language. Mark Ervine, son of David, was one of a group of four artists from Belfast who painted the huge Irish mural on the wall of the Flying Picket in New Bird Street when Liverpool was Capital of Culture in 2008. It included the statement : "An nasc idir Learpholl agus Éire : tá sé sa chultúr, sa stair agus san fhuil." (The link between Liverpool and Ireland : it's in the culture, in the history and in the blood.) Unfortunately the mural was painted over in 2013 by the proprietors of the Flying Picket club, where it was situated.

Linda Ervine, his aunt, is Irish Language Development Officer at the East Belfast Mission (Methodist) where she has facilitated Irish language classes since November 2011. In March, 2013, she was running five weekly classes for some 40 students at the Newtownards Road venue.

IRISH SPEAKERS IN OTHER PARTS OF BRITAIN

It was not just Liverpool that experienced an inflow of Irish-speaking migrants. Frederick Engels, in his book The Condition of the Working Class in England , From Personal Observation and Authentic Sources

[56] Runaghan, P. Father Nugent's Liverpool. Birkenhead 2003. P 14.

[57] Belchem, J. Irish, Catholic and Scouse. P 9

[58] Moffitt, M. ICM. MUP 2010. P 32

[59] O Snodaigh. P. Hidden Ulster . Dublin 1997. Pp 23-24

[60] Ibid Pp 28-29

[61] The Irish Times 16/1/2013 Article by Deaglán De Bréadún

(written 1844-1845) [62]has a section entitled Irish Immigration and says that it had been calculated that more than one million Irish people had immigrated into the country at that time (before the Famine) and around 50,000 more arrived each year. He said that they lived in great poverty in the great cities and gave estimates for their numbers : in London, 120,000; in Manchester, 40,00; in Liverpool, 34,000; Bristol, 24,000; Glasgow, 40,000; Edinburgh, 29,000. The figures had been compiled by Archibald Alison.

Engel's family owned a cotton mill in Manchester and so he was most knowledgeable about that city. Not surprisingly, he states that he had heard the "Irish-Celtic language" spoken in the most thickly populated parts of Manchester (p.123). Engels himself began to learn the language with the help of his Irish partner, Mary Burns, in Manchester. He apparently felt very at home in the company of Mary Burns and her family and this no doubt encouraged him to learn the language. She died of a heart attack in 1863, but her sister Elizabeth, also helped Engels to learn the language. He wrote to his friend, Karl Marx, in 1870, to tell him that he had learnt the language (in Manchester) but wished to improve his knowledge of it and asked Marx to find him an Irish grammar in London. The fact that Engels asked Marx to do this would indicate that there was a vibrant Irish scene in London. This is further illustrated by their interest and involvement in the Fenian movement in the 1860s.

Irish-speakers in London faced similar difficulties to those in Liverpool, including hostility from the English Catholic hierarchy and the education system. Lynn Hollen Lees in her book about the Irish in Victorian London , 'Exiles of Erin' points out that only five of the 106 priests in 1842 in the London diocese could speak Irish, and as in Liverpool, this deficiency created conflict between parishioners and the hierarchy : "The presence of an Irish-speaking priest was so unusual that an Irish congregation in 1853 fought the transference of one who they said could make 'the Truths of our Church ..... more forcible and more beautifully intelligible to our ears and hearts by clothing them in the language of our Fatherland.' Residual loyalties to the use of Irish for confessions and sermons continued to exist, but no provision for transmission of the language was made." In Lynn Hollen Lees' opinion, the Roman Catholic Church "the one institution that might have helped save the language" had no real interest in doing so.

What is significant about the above is that it would have been possible for Irish-speaking migrants to move from city to city speaking only their own language, as is evidenced by some of the case studies in this book. Such migrants would have included, for example, famine refugees walking from Liverpool to towns and cities throughout the north of England, and Irish speakers moving the other way from towns like Hull to Liverpool.

It was not just the cities which witnessed an influx of Irish people : every year thousands of seasonal agricultural workers would cross to Liverpool and march out of town to work in counties across the country. John Denvir says that they mainly came from Connaught and Donegal (both mainly Irish-speaking areas) :"I have seen them filling the breadth of Prescot Street, as they left the town, marching up like an army on foot to the various parts of England they were bound for." [63]MJ Whitty (1795-1873) described them as appearing to be " a remnant of the Celtic Irish" which was surely a reference to their Irish language.[64] The American writer Herman Melville (1819-91) was so struck by their appearance when he stayed in the city in 1839 that he incorporated a description of them into his 1849 novel Redburn, His First Voyage [65] (See appendix three.) Although these men generally returned home after the harvest, John Denvir describes, in 1851, meeting small groups of these Connaught harvesters who had settled in villages in places like Lincolnshire :"Of the old people who are left, some scarcely know any tongue but Irish..."[66] If this is what they were like after many years living in rural England, one can only conclude that most of them were monoglot Irish speakers when they got off the boat in Liverpool and set out on their trek across country.

In many cases the language was passed on to the second generation. Denvir describes meeting, in a remote Welsh village, an elderly Irish man who was born in Kent, his parents having been hop pickers. :"He spoke Irish with fluency. He said that for generations before his time the Irish had gone as 'hoppers' into Kent. Some were London-born Irish, as at present others came from Ireland and went back each

---

[62] Panther edition 1969. P189-90

[63] Denvir, J . Life Story of an Old Rebel. Liverpool 1910. P 35

[64] Qouted in Belchem, J. Irish Catholic and Scouse . p 30

[65] Quoted in Seed, D (ed) American Travellers in Liverpool. Liverpool UP 2008. P 109

[66] Denvir, J. The Irish in Britain. London 1894. P 154

year..." [67]Describing the large Irish community in the South Wales valleys, Denvir says :"You will hear the racy Munster tongue of the original immigrant, while the accent of his children and grandchildren is indistinguishable from that of their Welsh neighbours, whose vernacular they speak; indeed you will find some who can converse in all three tongues- Irish, Welsh and English."[68] In order to hear the confessions of the Irish speakers, Father Signini, an Italian priest working in South Wales in the 1850s , compiled a small Irish conversation book .[69]

It would be wrong to assume that the Irish language was confined to the labouring classes. I have already given examples of the language being used by some educated Protestants, and this was like-wise the case with many better-off, educated Catholics. Daniel O Connell (1775-1847) was brought up speaking Irish and passed the language on to his children. During his campaign for Catholic Emancipation (achieved in 1829) and his subsequent campaign for the repeal of the Act of Union, he would address rallies in Irish when his audience were non-English speakers and he reportedly spoke in Irish at the monster rally at Mullaghmast, Co. Kildare on October 1, 1843, to the dismay of the Government shorthand writer. [70] The Irish community on Merseyside was mobilised for the final monster meeting at Clontarf on October 8, a meeting which was banned by the government, with O'Connell being arrested.[71]

O'Connell was a frequent visitor to Liverpool, while en route to Parliament, and often stayed at the Adelphi Hotel. John Denvir describes being brought by his father to see O'Connell address a rally from the balcony of the Adelphi Hotel, and also seeing him at mass at Copperas Hill Chapel (St Nicholas') .[72] As a lawyer, and later an MP, he moved in English-speaking circles and in 1833 he erroneously stated that the use of Irish 'was diminishing among our peasantry'. O'Connell was a strong advocate of the transference to English speaking, at the expense of Irish. "Yes and I am sufficiently utilitarian not to regret its gradual abandonment.....Therefore, although the Irish language is connected with many recollections that twine around the hearts of Irishmen, yet the superior utility of the English tongue, as the medium of all modern communication, is so great, that I can witness without a sigh, the gradual disuse of Irish." [73] Hardly an argument for being bilingual.

His view in this matter can be contrasted with that of another lawyer/MP from the South West of Ireland : Edward Kenealy (1819-80). "He was one of the large number of Irish doctors, lawyers and writers who appeared when restrictions on Catholics receiving education and professional training were relaxed by the British Government." [74](This is a reference to the Catholic Relief Act of 1792) Like many in his generation he emigrated from Cork to London where he maintained his interest in the Irish language, at the same time becoming one of the most famous lawyers of his day. He joined the London Irish Confederation in 1847, took part in Chartist activities and became President of the Davis Club. He was elected MP for Stoke 1875-1880.

The great Irish scholar John O'Donovan studied law at Grays Inn, London, from 1844-1847. He spent his spare time researching in the libraries of Oxford, Lambeth and the British Museum, though he did not practice at the bar. His friend, the poet Dennis MacCarthy, also settled in London.[75] This tradition was carried on in the capital in the latter part of the nineteenth century, with the foundation of groups such as The Southwark Junior Irish Literary Society Club in 1881, which taught local Irish youngsters the Irish language and Irish history. A branch for adults was founded two years later, also by Frank Fahy, a native Irish -speaker from Co. Galway and in 1891 The London Irish Literary Society was established. From the latter group sprang the London Branch of the Gaelic League in 1894 and the Irish Texts Society , which was set up in 1898 to publish modern works in the Irish language.[76]

[67] Denvir, J. The Irish in Britain, 1894. P 79

[68] Denvir, J. The Irish in Britain 1894 p 306

[69] Beck, G. (ed) The English Catholics 1850-1950. London 1950. P 268

[70] Ryan, M. Fenian Memories. Dublin 1945 pp 130-131

[71] MacDonagh, O. O Connell. London 1991. P 520

[72] Denvir, J . Life Story of an Old Rebel. 1910. P 48

[73] MacDonagh, O. O Connell. London 1991. P 11

[74] Quinlivan,P & Rose, P.The Fenians in England London 1982. P 82

[75] Boyne, P. John O Donovan. Kilkenny 1987.p 107

[76] O Súilleabháin, d. Conradh na Gaeilge i Londain 1894-1917. Dublin 1989. P 6

The size of the literate Irish population living in Britain can be gauged from the huge sales of the Dublin Penny Journal which ran from 1832-1836. Its aim was to promote Irish literature, folklore, antiquities and the Irish language and it reached a circulation of 40,000 by its twentieth number. It was sold wholesale in London, Liverpool, Manchester, Birmingham, Edinburgh and Glasgow. James Clarence Mangan (pretending to be an Italian learning Irish) used an address in Clarence Street, Liverpool to write to the Journal to ask for advice about what books to study. John O'Donovan, who was a regular contributor, replied with the requested advice. Two-thirds of the sales of the journal were made outside of Ireland. [77]

Coincidentally, Daniel O'Connell died in 1847, at the height of the Famine, the event that more than anything else hastened the decline of the Irish language. His body lay in state aboard the steamship Duchess of Kent in the Mersey while en route back to Ireland. That same year, 300,000 other Irish-speakers made the opposite journey, landing in Liverpool in the hope of escaping the Great Hunger.

THE IMPACT OF THE GREAT HUNGER

The Famine caused hundreds of thousands of people to flee from Ireland. Cheap fares from Dublin to Liverpool, from where there were transatlantic services to America and Canada, meant that Merseyside became a popular destination. The influx did not go unnoticed and in December 1846 Edward Rushton, the stipendiary magistrate, ordered the police to count the numbers coming off the Irish vessels, which all arrived at Clarence Dock. According to their figures (quoted in Neal) 296,231 people arrived in 1847, of whom 50,000 (17%) were on business; 130,000 (44%) were emigrants and 116,231 (39%) were paupers who were "half naked and starving" according to Rushton in a letter to the Home Secretary .[78]

In 1847 Liverpool had shipping routes to Dublin, Drogheda, Cork, Wexford, Derry and Sligo as well as connections with other minor ports. "On one afternoon in August 1848, in excess of 1,200 destitute people left Waterford Quays for Liverpool."[79]

"The majority of famine refugees entering Britain through Liverpool came from the famine-stricken counties of the west coast of Ireland," says Neal and he mentions Counties Clare, Cork, Kerry, Galway, Mayo and Sligo in particular, with whole families of men, women and young children walking in excess of 150 miles to reach the Leinster ports of Drogheda and Dublin to embark, as fares were cheapest from these ports.

According to census of 1851 (the first to contain the question of language) the majority of people in the above mentioned counties were Gaelic speakers, with the proportion in many areas being over 80%. It follows therefore, that most of the Irish famine refugees arriving in Liverpool would have been Gaelic speakers, given that most of them came from these primarily Gaelic-speaking counties. Writing of the Great Famine, James Kelly states :"According to recent calculations approximately 1 million people died, of which an estimated 40 per cent came from Connacht, 30 per cent from Munster, 21 per cent from Ulster and 9 per cent from Leinster. Inevitably the crisis was most severe in the poorest areas...." [80] With regard to the Irish language he says that as the population had increased there were probably more Irish speaking people in the early nineteenth century than at any time before, but he adds that death and massive emigration decimated the language. But despite this, the 1851 census figures show the continuing strength of the language in the provinces of Connacht and Munster. The position of the Irish language would have been much stronger if one million people had not died and another million had not been forced to emigrate.

The figure for one million dead may well be a conservative one. The English historian, AJP Taylor (1906-1990) put the figure at "nearly two million " [81]. Cecil Woodham Smith argues that the 1841 census underestimated the size of the population of Ireland, due to local overcrowding, geographical difficulties and the unwillingness of the people to be registered. "In 1841 the population of Ireland was given as 8,175,124; in 1851, after the famine, it had dropped to 6,552,385, and the Census Commissioners calculated that, at the normal rate of increase, the total should have been 9,018,799, so that a loss of at

[77] Boyne, P. John O Donovan. Pp 51-55

[78] Neal. F. Black '47. Liverpool 1988. P 62

[79] McElwee, R. The Last Voyages of the Waterford Steamers, quoted in Morris, JM, Into the Crucible (Widnes) Birkenhead 2005

[80] Kelly, J in Atlas of Irish History (Duffy, S, ed) Dublin 1997 pp 92-95

[81] Taylor, AJP, Essays in 19th Century Europe. P 152

least 2.5 million persons had taken place." [82]

Gearóid Ó Tuathaigh points out that English was the language of the law, commerce, politics and increasingly the Catholic Church after the foundation of Maynooth, and so there was great pressure on ordinary people to abandon Gaelic. However, despite this, the absolute number of Irish speakers continued to rise up to 1845 due to population increase. "They were heavily concentrated, in class and regional terms, among the poorest sections of Irish society, and when the famine came they were decimated. Famine mortality was the highest among the cottier and labourer classes, the main custodians of the Irish language. In the diaspora that followed, the emigrant ship bound for Boston or Liverpool usually had a heavy quota of Irish speakers aboard." [83]

These people travelled from ports such as Dublin, Drogheda, Sligo, Derry, Waterford and Cork. The poorest of them were deck passengers which meant that they spent the entire length of the voyage- 12 hours- out on the open deck, often lashed by stormy seas. "In reference to the problem of overcrowding, Besnard (the general weight-master of Cork) stated that the fare from Cork to Liverpool was ten shillings, and he had witnessed a steamer carrying 1100 deck passengers and 300 pigs below decks. The fare for the pigs was half that for a passenger but the pigs were better looked after because they were of value to someone." [84] This book carries harrowing accounts of half-starved people freezing to death on the decks of these vessels. In the case of the steamer Londonderry, which sailed from Sligo to Liverpool in December 1848, 72 men, women and children suffocated or were trampled to death after having being forced into a small confined space below decks by the captain during a storm. (These were not the first Gaels to endure suffering and death on the River Mersey. 100 years previously, 936 men, women and children, rounded up in the wake of the 1745 uprising in Scotland, were shackled in pairs aboard a hulk on the Mersey prior to their transportation to the plantations of America and the Carribean Islands, where they were sold as indentured slaves. [85] Although some are on record as dying while in Liverpool, on the whole they were probably better looked after than the Irish famine refugees 100 years later because, like the animals, they were of value to someone.)

Although some of the adult male refugees who had worked as harvesters in the past might have passed through Liverpool before, for most of them, and particularly the women and children, it was probably their first sea voyage and their first visit to a foreign city. Hungry and exhausted after the long voyage, they disembarked at the Clarence Dock, where their appearance shocked many better-off English people :"In attire, in manners, in habits, in the wildness of look, of gesture, and of language, many of those who came recently over (among whom several who could not speak English at all) appeared to me to have more savagery about them, than can be included within the lowest definition of civilised life." [86] Despite the rather racist tone of his eye-witness account, the Rev Johns was to show the strength of his Christian beliefs later that year when he died from typhus contracted in "attending the body of a victim which, with the exception of a Catholic priest, no other person would touch." [87]

The fact that the majority of Irish people arriving in Liverpool during the Famine years were Gaelic speakers is illustrated by the case studies of refugees cited by Professor Neal :"John and Catherine Waters and their children, Patrick aged 16, Mary and Biddy, 14 year old twins, Anthony aged seven, Annie aged three and John aged one, all walked from Mayo to Drogheda," From there they took a steamer to Liverpool. "Significantly, John Waters could not speak English and his wife Catherine had never been to England in her life "In her words "...the want of potatoes, starvation and poverty obliged us to leave." [88] They had been evicted by Lord Darrens in October 1846 and their winter-walk of over 150 miles to catch the boat to Liverpool had taken nine days. From there the family walked 45 miles to Stockport, via Prescot and Warrington. "This was at a time when snow and frost was occurring. In addition, despite his lack of English, John Waters and some of the children went out begging." He eventually died of hunger and cold. Their aim had been to walk to Sheffield (across the Pennines in

[82] Woodhan Smith, C. The Great Hunger . London 1962. P 409

[83] O Tuathaigh, G. Ireland Before the Famine 1798-1840. Dublin 2007. P 41

[84] Neal, F. Black '47. P 73

[85] Higham, D. Liverpool and the '45 Rebellion. Countyvise, 1995. Pp 109-110

[86] Johns, J. Liverpool Domestic Mission Annual Report, 1847.

[87] Holt, RV. The Unitarian Contribution to Social Progress in England. London 1952. P 338

[88] Neal, F. Black '47. Pp 180-81

winter) where John Waters had a brother .They had hoped to find work in the factories for the children. When the son of John McQuinn died he was unable to give evidence to the coroner "as he did not speak English. Mary McQuinn aged 17 years, spoke for him ." They had walked 80 miles over the Pennine Hills, to Otley in North Yorkshire[89] Some of the refugees crossed over to Birkenhead, where many of them settled permanently, particularly in the Price Street area.

Others walked the 13 miles to Chester, where they mainly settled in the Irish quarter of Boughton. The Irish-born population of the city doubled in ten years , from 1,013 in 1841 to 2,032 in 1851. By 1867 it stood at 4,500 (estimate). [90]The arrival of so many very poor people, speaking a different language, made a big impact on the ancient city, although the Chester Chronicle was mainly sympathetic to their plight. It noted that the Irish population " had no claim upon the soil" of their own country, which was largely in the hands of the big landlords and middlemen. Significantly it stated that they had been classed as aliens "....just as Lord Lyndhurst designated them, as aliens in blood, religion and language." [91]

The fact that a regional English newspaper quoted the above statement 10 years after it was made in the House of Lords, shows its significance at the time. James Connolly (1868-1916) the Edinburgh-born son of Irish speaking refugees used the same quotation from Lord Lyndhurst in his analysis of the famine in his book, Labour and Irish History. In the chapter entitled 'The Sacrifice of the Peasantry' he describes the huge mortality rates in Ireland at a time when vast quantities of food were being exported, something which the British Government of the day justified as they rigorously imposed the rules of the free market economy. Those in the British establishment who regarded the Irish as "aliens in blood, language and religion," attempted to rationalise such inhumane policy on that basis.[92]

It is clear then, that most of the refugees were either bilingual or else monoglot Irish speakers. Most of them were very poor and left behind no record of their experiences. We are fortunate that we know a lot about the life of two at least of these refugees. Firstly, Micheál Dáibhéid (1846-1906) or Michael Davitt as he was known in English. He was to achieve fame as founder of the Land League and was elected to Parliament for South Mayo in 1895. He was the second of the five children of Martin and Catherine Davitt. In 1850 the entire family was evicted from their home by Lord Lucan, because of rent arrears. The bailiffs set fire to the roof of their peasant cottage in Sráid, Co. Mayo and the family walked over 150 miles across country to Dublin to get the boat to Liverpool. Michael Davitt was four years old. The youngest child was two months old and it was November. From Liverpool they walked 50 miles to the mill town of Haslingden in Lancashire where they joined the already-established Irish -speaking community of Rock Hall. "All his neighbours were Irish and many were unable to speak English. Davitt was, of course, an Irish speaker." [93] St Mary's Catholic Church in Haslingden was built in 1859 to cater for the huge Irish influx and was staffed by Irish-speaking priests.

Another who has left a first-hand account of events was Marcas O Roighin (Mark Ryan,1844-1940). As a child he was evicted with his family on three separate occasions from small farms in Galway. "My longest recollection is to see my father and mother, brothers and sisters thrown on the roadside- a bitter and humiliating experience which we suffered on three successive occasions."[94] They eventually crossed to Liverpool in 1860 and settled near Bacup, which is not far from Haslingden. They too were Irish speakers and Mark Ryan was initiated into the IRB by Davitt in 1865. Mark Ryan returned to Galway in 1867 and studied at St Jarlath's College in Tuam, where he was taught by Fr Ulick Burke, who was to play an important role in the Irish language movement in the north west of England, as we will see later. Mark Ryan eventually trained as a doctor. He ended up working back in the north west of England, where he spent time in Liverpool as an agent for the Fenians. He then moved on to Wales and eventually to London (from 1882 to 1924) where his brother Patrick also practised as a doctor. Together with their sister, Maighréad, they became prominent members of the Gaelic League in London. They never lost their love of their native language, despite all the hardships they went through as a family, and neither did they turn their back on it when they became professional people in the English capital.

[89] Neal, F. Black '47. P 187

[90] Cheshire History no 51, 2011-12. Cheshire Local History Association.

[91] The Chronicle, Chester. 19/3/1847. The Irish Poor Law

[92] Connolly, J. Labour in Irish History. 1910

[93] Dunleavy, J. Michael Davitt's Haslinden. Irish Post 30/6/1984

[94] Ryan, M. Fenian Memories. Dublin 1945. P 1

Despite having his right arm amputated when aged 11 years after it was crushed while he worked as a machine minder in a mill, Michael Davitt managed to acquire an education and employment with the help of local people. As Irish was the everyday language of the community in which he lived, Davitt was bilingual and when, as an adult, he spoke at Land League meetings in the West of Ireland, Irish was the language he used. "Arís agus arís eile, tharraing sé aird a chuid éisteoirí ar thábhacht na Gaeilge, rud a bhí an-neamhchoitianta go deo in óráidí ceannairí pobal." "Again and again he drew the attention of his audiences to the importance of the Irish language, something which was most uncommon in speeches by public leaders."[95]

He continued this theme in the USA, and at a famous speech before thousands in the Mechanics Hall in Boston, December 8, 1878, he spoke of the importance of the language in helping the people to maintain their identity. When Davitt was imprisoned in February 1883 for making what were considered seditious speeches, he taught his fellow-prisoner T.M. Healy how to speak Irish. [96] When Davitt spoke Irish he used the Mayo dialect of his family, but when he spoke English it was with a Lancashire accent, indicating that he spoke Irish at home, but English with neighbours. This is not an uncommon occurrence. Many Irish speakers in Donegal, for example, speak English with a Glasgow accent.

Haslingden was a typical Lancashire mill town which had expanded from being a large village of 4,000 in 1801 to 10,000 by the time the Davitt's arrived. About a 1000 (10% of the population) were Irish. [97] There was a certain amount of religious and social animosity towards the Irish migrants, (including an attack by a mob on the chapel) which no doubt encouraged them to live together in Rock Hall and nearby streets such as Wilkinson Street. This would help explain why the Irish language survived as a community language in the town, in rather the same way that Asian languages persist in similar towns today. Haslingden may be regarded as a much smaller-scale version of Liverpool.

Martin Davitt, Michael's father, had run a hedge school in Mayo. He conducted a school for local Irish children in his home in Haslingden. He also worked as an agent for the Friendly Society of St Patrick which meant that he made contact with the Irish community in surrounding towns like Accrington and Blackburn. The society was based in Liverpool, so he would also have been in contact with the Irish community there. Its manager was John Treacy, who had worked in an ancillary capacity in the Irish Ordnance Survey (1830-1842). This is interesting on two counts : firstly, Richard O' Donovan, the son of the Irish scholar John O' Donovan (1801-61) who advised on place names during the survey, came to live in Liverpool in 1875 and because of this connection the local branch of the Gaelic League is named The John O' Donovan branch. Secondly, the Irish Ordnance Survey was used as the backdrop in Brian Friel's play Translations, which has, as its main themes, the impact of a colonial power upon an indigenous culture and the cultural detriment which comes with the loss of a language. The play was staged in Liverpool in 2005.

Michael Davitt had Liverpool connections. He acted as a mediator during the dock strike in Liverpool in 1889 and he was friends with a number of Irish-language activists from the city, notably Stiofán MacEnna (1872-1934). (See later section on their visit to Tolstoy.)

HOW LARGE WAS THE IRISH SPEAKING COMMUNITY IN LIVERPOOL?

According to the Medical Officer of Health's report on Irish Immigration, of the 300,000 Irish migrants who landed in 1847 "60,000 to 80,000 have located themselves amongst us." (see later section on the Hume survey of Irish speakers.) Many of these people are on record as still using the Irish language years later. For example, the Liverpool Catholic Herald newspaper February 20 1909 recorded the golden wedding anniversary of Mr and Mrs Maxwell from County Mayo, who were fluent Irish speaking famine migrants who had met and married in Liverpool. [98] Assuming that they came to Liverpool in 1850, the fact that they were still using Irish 50 years later is an indication of its strength as a community language and the fact that they told the newspaper about it would indicate that they were proud of the fact. They would appear to have had a very similar outlook to that of Michael Davitt as regards the Irish language.

George Brown, the head of the Catholic Church in Lancashire who had declined to employ Irish priests, was sympathetic to the plight of the Irish poor when news of the distress caused by the famine began to

[95] Mac Aonghusa, P. Ar Son na Gaeilge. Dublin 1993. P34

[96] King, C. Michael Davitt. UCD 2009 p 44

[97] Dunleavy, J. Davitt's Haslingden. Haslingden 2006.

[98] Quoted in Belcham, J. Irish, Catholic and Scouse.p 190

reach Liverpool. In January 1847 he issued a circular to all parishes in Lancashire announcing a collection for the famine victims in Ireland. Nearly £5,000 was raised through church collections and subscriptions from wealthy individuals. This money was sent to Bishops McHale and Slattery in the west and south of Ireland respectively, as distress was worst in these areas.

However Brown, like the Unitarian minister Rev Johns, was horrified at the huge increase in famine refugees landing in Liverpool and was most un-Christian in his comments about them. He reported to Rome that "the dreadful plague which the poor Irish have brought into our cities- they are immersed in starvation and squalor- has upset almost everything that related to religion and the clergy." [99]By way of contrast, Fr Luigi Gentili reported to Rome that Brown had a fine country house (Bishop Eton) near Liverpool "and a carriage, servants male and female."

The ordinary Catholic priests showed great bravery in attending to the Irish fever victims. Ten out of the 24 priests in Liverpool died in this way in 1847, as did two Irish Christian Brothers who taught in poor areas of the city. So also did the Rev Johns and ten medical practitioners. The Irish Christian Brothers may well have been acting as interpreters for the priests, who were nearly all English. This is a role that they already carried out in Ireland. Two priests also died of fever in Wigan in 1848. This left George Brown with a chronic shortage of priests, particularly Irish-speaking ones. He wrote to All Hallows College in Dublin begging for some Irish priests. He had little success, however, as America and Australia were also competing for them and they were few in number.

In this desperate situation the ordination at Ushaw Seminary in Durham, of 23-year old Irishman Father (later Bishop) Bernard O' Reilly was brought forward urgently. He was appointed to St Patrick's in Liverpool to fill the gap left by the demise of the first of the three priests to die there. The fact that he could speak Irish would have been a huge advantage when it came to visiting the sick and hearing confession. He himself caught the fever in the course of his duties, but recovered.

Pierse Power (1823-1895) was ordained at St John's College, Waterford, for the Lancashire District in June 1847 and was appointed curate at St Patrick's, Liverpool. He became the first Irish parish priest at St Anthony's (1859-68) and later served at St John's Kirkdale, until his death in March 1895. His nephew, Patrick O'Donovan (1834-1915) who was also from Waterford, trained at Maynooth and was appointed as a curate at St Joseph's, Grosvenor Street, off Scotland Road, in 1870. He moved to St Brigid's later that year. Like his uncle, he delivered sermons in Irish, something that was commented on by visitors from Ireland during the Gaelic revival later in the century.

The Irish who settled in Liverpool congregated around St Patrick's church in the South End and St Anthony's in the North End. Not only were there existing Irish communities in these areas -which meant there was less chance of hostility from resentful locals - but they were also close to the docks which employed large numbers of casual workers. It was the North End, though, that was to expand into the primary Irish enclave in the city, famously electing an Irish nationalist MP, TP O 'Connor, in 1885. He held the seat until his death in 1923. For monoglot Irish speakers, or for people whose first language was Irish, being amongst people with whom they could converse easily was obviously a major attraction, especially as this community was to be served by Irish speaking priests and doctors and even Protestant clergymen in the years to come.

THE LIVERPOOL GAELTACHT

As I showed in Chapter one, there were clearly thousands of Irish speaking people living in Liverpool prior to the famine, evidenced by the petition requesting more Irish-speaking priests.

The famine period, 1845-1852 brought over one million Irish people to Liverpool, the majority of whom, I would argue, would either have had Irish as their first language or else would have had at least a knowledge of the language. Most of these migrants passed through the city either by ship to America or Canada or else on foot to other places in England. I have looked at some case studies of the latter - for example the Davitt family - and referred to one case study of a family - the Maxwells- who stayed in Liverpool and kept on speaking the language. But how many more were there like them? The Medical Officer of Health estimated that 60,000 to 80,000 Irish migrants opted to stay in Liverpool in 1847. When this number was added to the existing Irish-speaking population, there must have been a very large Gaelic speaking community indeed.

---

[99] Doyle. P. Mitres & Missions in Lancashire. P 40 & 56

When I discussed this topic with Frank Neal, he kindly sent me further case studies, and also recommended that I look at the book : Missions at Home, or A clergyman's account of a portion of the Town of Liverpool by the Rev Abraham Hume, 1850, as he had made use of the book himself.

Abraham Hume (1814-1884) was from Hillsborough, Co. Down and was vicar in Vauxhall, (North Liverpool), from 1847 till his death in 1884. He was both an explorer and historian who wrote more than 100 books and pamphlets, as well as articles in the Ulster Journal of Archaeology (which promoted the Irish language). He was keen to use statistical techniques to analyse the religious practices of the community in which he lived.[100]

In Missions at Home he describes the spiritual state of the population of Vauxhall and the neighbouring area of St Stephens. On page 32 he says :

"25- The statistics of the Irish-speaking population have been taken.

26-Several copies of portions of the New Testament in Irish, have been distributed among the people. These were kindly supplied to me by the late Mr Langtry.

27- Four persons who could speak the language were taught to read it. It was thought that in their intercourse, casual or designed, some good might be done to others; and portions of the Irish Scriptures were placed in the hands of these individuals to enable them to turn their knowledge to a useful account.

28- I commenced to learn the language myself, in the hope of being able to establish a Church Service in Irish.

I should have been able to preach in the language; but it was found on inquiry that the Irish-speaking Protestants were scarcely 1 in 100 of the whole, so that it would have been impossible, within such narrow limits, to form a regular congregation from among them. I then applied to the Secretary and Treasurer of the Liverpool Auxiliary Irish Society, and earnestly urged the appointment of an Irish reader (out of the funds collected in Liverpool,) whose attention might be, in a great degree, given to these two districts of the town. It is probable that some step would have been taken in the matter, but the sudden and lamented death of Mr Langtry, the Treasurer, occurred a few days after the receipt of my letter."

Hume states that every Protestant family in the area was visited by a lay scripture reader and given a leaflet about Church of England services. It was found that some of them could not read and "others again can neither read nor speak English." Assuming that these people were Irish, it would appear that there were some monoglot Irish speaking Protestants living in Liverpool, which fits in with my observations in Chapter one about Irish-speaking Protestant communities in Ireland. Hume does distinguish between Protestants i.e. Church of England members and Dissenters, as he states that there was one Dissenting chapel in Vauxhall, in which the services were all in Welsh, to cater for about 500 Welsh dissenting Protestants in the area.

According to his statistics, out of 1580 Catholic households in the St Stephens district, 869 of them spoke Irish and 711 English. His analysis covers every street. For example, in Lace Street, out of 89 households, 78 were Irish speaking. Narrow passage-ways, running off Lace Street, led into 25 courts which housed another 90 families, of whom 75 were Irish-speaking. So the population of this short street and its adjoining courts was a staggering 1,110 people, comprising 179 families of whom 153, or 85.5%, were Irish-speaking. This would clearly represent a strong, sustainable community from a linguistic point of view. Most of the other 51 streets and 422 courts in St Stephens and Vauxhall contained a number of Irish speaking families, so it would have been possible to have lived in the area and socialised in Irish on a daily basis. In this community it would have been perfectly feasible for monoglot Irish speakers, or people with very little English, to have got by.

In the district of Vauxhall, out of 1142 families, 487 of them spoke Irish and 655 English.

Karen P, Corrigan [101]in her essay examines the pressures that encouraged Irish emigrants to abandon their language and 'teach English to the children.' Presumably the same pressure applied in Liverpool. That is, many Irish speaking parents would have opted to speak English at home, in front of the children, so that they could advance themselves in Liverpool. So I would argue that most, if not all, of the families listed in Hume's survey, could speak Irish as well as English but opted for the latter in order to gain social/

[100] Hume Papers. D 27656. Public Record Office of Northern Ireland. www.proni.gov.uk

[101] Corrigan, P in : The Irish in the New Communities (O Sullivan,P, ed) Leicester UP 1992

economic advancement in a strange land. Finding and holding on to a job, or working as a street trader or even begging, all would require at least some knowledge of English. At the same time, the large number of Irish speakers inevitably had an effect on the dialect of English spoken locally. (see later section)

Hume's survey provides hard contemporary statistical data from an impartial source (i.e. someone who could not be accused of being an Irish nationalist with an axe to grind). The districts covered by Hume's survey were particularly badly hit by the fever epidemic which struck the famine refugees in 1847-48. In Lace Street, which had the highest number of Irish speakers in the Hume Survey, one third of the inhabitants -that is 472 persons - died from fever during that year. "During 1847, 60,000 were treated for typhus and another 40,000 for dysentery and diarrhoea. Of this total of 100,000, 8,500 died and the highest death rates were in the Irish wards of Vauxhall, Scotland and Exchange." [102]

The typhus epidemic was almost over by February 1848, but there were still numerous cases of death by starvation. Then in December of that year a cholera epidemic began. This epidemic caused 5,245 deaths in 1849 and again it was the Irish districts covered by the Hume survey which were worst hit. Burke estimates that 15,000 people, mostly Irish, died from hunger or fever in Liverpool during this period.[103] Clearly, staying alive- for Irish speakers - was not easy, either in Ireland or Liverpool, and it is little wonder that the survival of the language itself was under threat.

The Catholic clergy were well-aware of Hume's survey. Thomas Burke refers to it twice in Catholic History of Liverpool, which was published in Liverpool in 1910.[104] He quotes statistics from "a census taken by a well-known Anglican clergyman, Canon Hume, who made a house to house visit.." But the statistics he quotes are to do with the poverty and lack of education provision for Irish children, not the fact that they spoke Gaelic. Later on, Burke states : "an interesting pamphlet was published not long since by a distinguished clergyman of the Established Church (Canon Hume)" but he uses the findings of the survey to illustrate the poverty and crime in the Vauxhall area in which the Sisters of Notre Dame had successfully started up a school.

The fact that Burke does not refer to Gaelic being spoken by the Irish in Liverpool may be due to the fact that it was considered 'normal' that Irish people would speak Irish and therefore not worth commenting on. This phenomenon is discussed in the book The Irish Language in the United States by TW Ihde and also in an essay by Brian McGinn [105].He provides a number of examples of the language being used in America in the 19th century and states : "For Irish observers, the sight of Irish athletes playing hurling was not news. And with rare exceptions, the sound of Irish emigrants speaking Irish was likewise not deemed noteworthy by their fellow emigrants." Burke's Irish roots lay in Conamara - one of the strongest Irish speaking areas in the country - and so he would have regarded it as normal for other Irish immigrants to speak the language.

THE IRISH LANGUAGE – A VEHICLE FOR CONVERSION?

Burke's reticence about the Irish language may have arisen out a sense of shame about the huge number of supposed converts from Conamara claimed by the Irish-speaking agents of the ICM. This was certainly the case with Archbishop MacHale, who appeared to be in denial about their work in his area.[106] It is likely that the intense poverty of the people was a more important issue for Burke, than the language they spoke, which is understandable. In addition, there was no doubt concern that Hume's interest in the subject was motivated by a desire to convert the poor Catholic Irish to Protestantism. This type of issue helped to create an ambivalent attitude on the part of some Catholic leaders towards Gaelic : they were pleased that most speakers of the language were Catholics but they were suspicious of the motives of non-Catholics who took an interest in Gaelic. I will refer to a number of examples of this later.

Rev Hume makes reference to the Liverpool Auxiliary Irish Society. This was part of the Irish Society (IS) referred to in chapter one, which was founded in Dublin in 1818 " for promoting the education of the native Irish through the medium of their own language" and intended to "afford the same advantages for education to all classes of professing Christians."[107] Moffit states that the IS taught the Irish-speaking

[102] Neal, F. Black '47. Ch 5

[103] Burke, T, Catholic History of Liverpool 1910. P 87

[104] Ibid. pp 89 & 103

[105] McGinn, B. www.irishdiaspora.net 2001

[106] Moffitt, M. ICM. P 97

[107] Ibid. p 29

peasantry to read, using the Irish bible as a textbook. It confined itself to educational methods and its policy was to employ Catholics in the schools it established. Although it was not overtly trying to convert Catholics to Protestantism, IS members hoped that by enabling Catholics to read the word of God for themselves, there might be positive results :

"The IS was unworried by its slow progress and allowed its scholars to remain Catholic, saying that few 'as far as we can learn, leave Romanism; but who can tell the blessed effects of the study of that Word to multitudes of such persons.'"

At its peak, in 1861, the IS maintained 68 missions in 12 counties from Waterford to Donegal, but was most active in Munster. It employed 74 scripture readers, 17 teachers and 239 'Irish teachers' who had over 8,000 pupils, while 500 scholars attended its 17 mission schools. This softly softly approach was in stark contrast to the Society for Irish Church Missions (ICM) and the Achill Mission (AM), which merged in 1852. Their approach was to offer food and clothing to the starving peasants in exchange for converting. Some ICM supporters saw the Famine as a heaven-sent opportunity. [108]They too needed the Irish language in order to communicate with the peasantry. The 'Soupers' as they were known, were denounced by the Catholic clergy and disliked by many clerics in the Church of Ireland who did not want confrontation with their Catholic counterparts. Nor did they want large numbers of poor peasants entering their ranks. An attempt to merge the IS and ICM failed in 1856.

Unlike the IS, the ICM was essentially an English organisation with little empathy with ordinary Irish people. As thousands of Irish migrants flooded into England and Scotland it was felt by many Protestants that an organisation like the ICM was needed in Britain. The Edinburgh Irish Mission (EIM) was founded in 1842 to oppose the advance of 'Popery' and to reach out to the Catholics. In order to do the latter, it employed Irish-speaking teachers. "The EIM was soon operative outside Scotland, with agents working among the Catholic populations of London, Liverpool and other cities..." [109]

"Speakers of Scots Gaelic were employed to deal with Celtic popery 'of both our own Highlands and of Ireland.' In the 1850s, the ICM would send Irish-speaking agents to work among Irish Catholics in Glasgow, although it is unclear whether they functioned independently or under the auspices of a Scottish Society."[110]

The ICM had its supporters in Liverpool, says Moffit, and quotes from a sermon given by the radical Irish Protestant Hugh M'Neile, entitled 'The famine, a rod of God, its provoking cause- its merciful design ' preached in St Judes Church, Liverpool Sunday February 2, 1847. He reminded his congregation that "Plagues, pestilences, famines.....(were) national punishments for sin". He did, however, urge them to contribute to famine relief collections.[111]

The fact that organisations like the ICM and ECM used the Irish language to try and win converts amongst the Irish both in Ireland and in places like Liverpool and Scotland seems to have acted against the language in the long term, by creating a negative attitude towards it on the part of some Catholics. "The EIM, like the ICM, rejoiced in the conversion of Catholic priests such as James Forbes, who joined the Free Church of Scotland and became an active missionary. His superintendent, the Irish-speaking Revd Patrick M'Menemy, was a convert of the Presbyterian Church in Ireland." [112]

Some Catholic leaders – including John McHale - remained positive about the Irish language, despite the tactics of the ICM. MacHale had considerable contact with the IS when he was bishop of Killala (1825-34), as the society was very active in north Mayo. He was, of course, aware of the famous sermon given by Archbishop William Magee in Dublin in 1822 when he claimed that the Church of Ireland possessed sole ecclesiastical legitimacy and thus started the 'Bible War' between the Catholics and evangelicals. This may have encouraged MacHale to begin his translation of the New Testament into Irish, but debates about theology were of little interest to the Irish poor, particularly those who spoke Irish. The biggest boost to the Presbyterian and IS missions in Mayo came from MacHale's exclusion of national schools from the Killala diocese as the missions then stepped in and taught the Irish peasantry to read, using the

---

[108] Ibid. P 54

[109] Ibid. pp 15-16

[110] ibid

[111] Moffitt, M. ICM p 54

[112] Ibid p 15

Irish bible as a textbook :"the people began with no other desire than to hear the Irish, but by-and-by the work of God rubbed off the scales and they saw the light, at first dimly, then more clearly."[113]

When this was done in areas where the English language was encroaching, it provided an excuse for Catholic priests who disliked the Irish language to rail against it. In 1836 John O'Donovan reported from Ballyjamesduff, Co. Cavan that : "the teachers of the bible through the medium of the Irish language have created in the minds of the peasantry a hatred of everything written in that language, and....the society who encourage them could not have adopted a more successful plan to induce them to learn English and hate their own language."[114]

As he wandered around the county, dressed all in black, talking Irish and doing his Ordnance Survey work, he was often mistaken for a bible teacher "who intends to make Protestants of the townlands." This made his work all the more difficult : "I can assure you that I was refused lodgings in several places in consequence of looking so like a swaddling preacher."[115] What comes across in Moffit's book is that the main concern of the Catholic church was to keep Catholics, and especially children, away from ICM missions, orphanages, schools etc. "Most of all, Catholic clergy feared the influence of Irish or text teachers "[116] Promoting the Irish language was not a particular concern of the Catholic clergy- their main concern was holding on to their flock This attitude mirrors that of Thomas Burke who repeatedly refers to the need to 'save' Catholic children from Protestant orphanages but only alludes to the separate culture of Irish speaking people occasionally . Burke himself was educated by the Irish Christian Brothers at St Vincent's School in Liverpool. Quite apart from their Catholicism, Irish people were in danger of losing, and often did lose, their rich linguistic and cultural heritage.

Although Burke does not criticise the work of Abraham Hume, he does make reference to " proselytisers" being active amongst the famine refugees and describes a ragged school which they opened in Hodson Street, off Byrom Street .."and with liberal offers of food and clothing tempted the poor children to enter its doors. Some few did succumb to the temptation, and were promptly taught the necessity of abandoning the 'errors of Rome.'"[117] Nearly half of the 51 families living in Hodson Street are listed as Irish-speaking in Hume's survey, as are the majority of the 68 families living in the seven adjacent courts. Working among such people was the modus operandi of the ICM and as such met with swift and direct opposition from the Catholic Church. Burke describes "the poverty-stricken famine immigrants, who had not as yet shaken off the terrors of 1847," and says that two priests, Fathers Noble and Egan, organised an open-air meeting in front of the Ragged School. "They then forced their way into the building, and bore away in triumph a number of Catholic children, on whose temporary 'conversion' the proselytisers had spent a considerable sum of money. This exploit put new life and courage into the poor wretches who had daily to face the dreadful alternative of food and the Authorised Version, or hunger and the faith of their fathers." Again, Burke makes no mention of what language was being used in the Ragged School, but given that the pupils enticed inside were poor famine refugees, it may very well have been Irish. It is likely that they did not see the offer of free food, clothing and education as "a dreadful alternative" to hunger, but rather as charity provided by people who spoke their own language.

As stated earlier, the lack of interest on the part of the Catholic Church in the Irish language, often fostered a lack of interest in the formal practice of Catholicism on the part of Irish-speaking Catholics and left the way open to Protestant Irish speakers looking for converts. For example, PT MacGinley (1857-1942) who was brought up in an Irish-speaking area of County Donegal and went on to become president of Conradh na Gaeilge/The Gaelic League describes how at Catholic chapel, both sermons and Catechism were in English, and that "both were unintelligible owing to the use of technical English words."[118] He and the rest of his brothers and sisters attended a National School, where, in common with all other National Schools, all the lessons were in English and Irish was not on the syllabus. The only Irish book he could get hold of was Bedell's Protestant Bible. He attempted to teach himself to read from that. He did this voluntarily and certainly did not regard it as "dreadful." Similarly, his mother, who worked as an Irish reader for a travelling teacher from a Protestant Society in order to earn fees, was fined in

[113] Ibid. P 29

[114] O Snodaigh, P. Hidden Ulster. Dublin 1997. P 16

[115] Boyne, P. John O Donovan. P 34

[116] Moffitt, M. ICM. P 123

[117] Burke, T. Catholic History of Liverpool. P 108

[118] In : The Voice of Ireland. Fitzgerald, WG (ed) Dublin 1938 . p 445

confession for this apparent 'offence.' Presumably it was she who provided her son with the Bedell Bible. "Throughout this period Church preaching and teaching was done almost wholly in English" says MacGinley. Clearly, if the Catholic Church had made more effort to disseminate MacHale's Irish language New Testament and to teach its doctrines in Irish, then it would not have faced such problems from proselytisers. The Catholic Church did not produce a complete Bible in Irish until 1981 so any Catholics wishing to read the Old Testament in Irish had to use the Bedell version. Eamonn De Valera apparently bought a copy from the Hibernian Bible Society during the Troubles .[119]

When the ICM provided free food and clothing to entice the starving, the Catholics did the same :"Catholic activists realised that the most effective answer to Protestant missionary activity was the distribution of food and clothing, the provision of free schooling and the establishment of alternative Catholic facilities for destitute children in areas of extreme poverty".[120]

Thus the Hodson Street Ragged School incident led the Catholic Church to raise money to build a school for the poor children of the area. Fontenoy Street Schools were opened in January 1854. The foundation stone had been laid by Fr James Nugent in 1852. To aid the work of giving religious instruction to the boys, and presumably to combat the efforts of Protestant organisations like the ICM, a branch of the Christian Doctrine Society was founded in the area. This consisted of laymen who taught the children Catechism on Sundays.[121] Burke does not mention which language they used, but given the huge numbers of Irish speakers in this area (as shown in Hume's survey) they would have needed to know something of the language to get their message across. The Vincentians (the largely Irish-speaking order of priests, dedicated to working with the poor) argued that the formation of branches of lay organisations like the Christian Doctrine Society was essential in the fight-back against the proselytisers.[122]

It is significant that the Ragged School incident took place at a time when the Irish Christian Brothers had been running a school in nearby St Anthony's, Scotland Road, since 1845. It had been run by lay teachers when it was established in 1841 as there were no Brothers available to work there, but by 1845 all the large Catholic schools for poor boys in Liverpool were being staffed by Brothers. Fourteen teaching Brothers were working in the city, living in four separate communities and teaching about 1,500 boys in six day schools. They also taught hundreds of adults in night schools. They appear to have had little free time as they were also closely involved in the community, leading the Rosary in St Patrick's Church, for example, and preparing adults and converts for the reception of the Sacraments.[123] Their knowledge of Irish would have been vital in bringing Catholic teaching to the speakers of that language, who had been seriously neglected by the largely English-speaking leadership of Maynooth in Ireland. Doyle cites a level of practice amongst Irish speakers as low as 20-40 per cent. This group had been similarly neglected by the English-born hierarchy of the church in Lancashire, as evidenced by the petition supported by Dr Butler in 1842.

The Vatican was well-aware of these issues : as mentioned earlier, Fr Gentili had reported on the neglect of the Irish-speaking Catholics in England. They also had a separate channel of information from Liverpool/Ireland : the Cullens. They wrote regularly to their brother, Father Paul Cullen (1803-1878), rector of the Irish College in Rome, who fulfilled the function of the Irish hierarchy's official agent there. His family members in Liverpool appraised him both of family matters and also of Church and the politics within it. For example, Thomas Cullen wrote to him in May 1843 to tell him that the dispute between Dr Butler (who had supported the petition regarding a lack of Irish-speaking priests in Liverpool) and Bishop George Brown was over. When Cullen visited Ireland he stayed with family members in Liverpool en route. In May 1845, for example, he received a letter addressed to him in Liverpool, from Fr Tobias Kirby (1804-1895) the Waterford-born Vice Rector of the Irish College in Rome. Later that year, Thomas Cullen wrote to Paul in Rome to tell him of the potato blight.[124]

Cullen, who was competent in several languages, had a copy of O'Donovan's Irish Grammar (published in 1845) sent out to him in November 1846 by Fr M. O'Sullivan of St Vincent's Seminary, Cork, together

[119] Mistéil, P (ed) The Irish Language and the Unionist Tradition. Belfast 1994. P 30

[120] Moffitt, M. ICM. P 117

[121] Burke, T. Catholic History of Liverpool. Pp 108-109

[122] Moffitt, M. ICM p 120

[123] Gillespie, W. The Christian Brothers in England, 1825-1880. Bristol 1975. P 104

[124] Papers of Paul Cullen. www.irishcollege.org

with a report on famine deaths in the area. This clearly shows he had a special interest in the Irish language and appreciated the role of the Vincentians in using the language to propagate the faith. The following year, his nephew Hugh (son of Thomas) wrote from Liverpool to describe the famine refugees, 3000 of whom were landing per day "fever among them." Cullen also received numerous reports about the proselytisers from Donegal down to Dingle. The nuns in Dingle Convent, for instance, who had earlier petitioned for funds for an orphanage, wrote to him :"Irish is the native language of the majority of children at school here." (13/11/1847)

Paul Cullen was in Liverpool and Ireland from August to November 1847. In a letter reminiscent of that of Fr Gentili in 1842 regarding Liverpool , he wrote to Tobias Kirby in Rome from Liverpool describing the neglect of Catholics in Conamara (which was later taken advantage of by the ICM) :"I hear several parishes are vacant, and no priest can be found to fill them, being unwilling to face the hardships."[125]

The educational and charitable work of Fr Nugent and the Irish Jesuit Fr O' Carroll can be viewed in the context of the Catholic fight-back against the proselytisers. Fr Nugent founded his first Ragged School for 200 children in Liverpool in 1849. This was followed by Fr O Carroll at SFX in 1853. Here free clothing was distributed to the poorest pupils and meals were served to about 150 children per day, provided they had attended mass on the previous Sunday.[126] It would be wrong, of course, to suggest that the primary motive of the priests was to combat the work of the proselytisers of the ICM. In 1847, when Fr Nugent was working in Blackburn as a newly-ordained priest, he organised a collection for the Irish Fund which had been set up to help the Famine refugees. This was before the foundation of the ICM in 1849, the year he set up his first ragged school in Spitalfields, Liverpool. There were seven ragged schools operating in the city in 1849. A decade later there were 32, run by a variety of religious groups. Fr John Furnival states that although the schools were meant to be non-denominational in theory, they were in fact symbols of the religious divide.[127] This fits in with Moffitt's thesis that the poorest of Ireland's inhabitants-the peasantry of Conamara and the slum-dwellers of Dublin- found themselves as pawns in the power struggle between the ICM and the Catholic Church. As thousands of these people crossed over to Liverpool, they found themselves in the same position.

Although the appeal of the ICM diminished with the end of the famine in 1852, the on-going poverty of the people, on both sides of the Irish Sea, saw it continue to attract clients from the Catholic community. The anonymity and mobility of city dwellers meant that they were less vulnerable to the campaign of social ostracism conducted by the Catholic clergy against 'jumpers' as they were called. In Dublin, as late as 1880, two Sunday classes for Irish speakers were held in the ICM Coombe School and in December 1898 the London Committee of the organisation introduced a mandatory Irish examination for all candidates from the west of Ireland entering its Training School

The Catholic Church in Liverpool clearly monitored the activities of the ICM. Fr William Pinnington, who was secretary of the Catholic Children's Aid Society (1899-1909) is described as waiting on the Liverpool Landing Stage for a group of Irish children :"who were subject to an act of proselytising when a group allocated them to a Protestant home for children in England....He went on board and rounded up the children in the very presence of the group that had brought them and escorted them to a Catholic Home."[128] The 'group' was probably the ICM. We are not told what the children made of the escapade but we are given a clue from another story about two young boys in a Catholic Home who were transferred to a non-Catholic Institution by a relative. Fr Pinnington tracked the boys down. They were interviewed privately, to come to a decision about which home they really wanted to go to, while Pinnington waited outside. "Fr Pinnington meanwhile paced up and down, saying the rosary. One boy was asked why they finally decided in favour of the Catholic one ; his answer was -"because the grub's better!"

Although English, Fr Pinnington became very sympathetic to the cultural needs of the Irish community in the Scotland Road area of Liverpool, where he worked at St Alphonsus. He was behind the opening of St Alphonsus School, Stanley Road in 1889 and when the Liverpool branch of the Gaelic League was established in 1896 he was an enthusiastic supporter of its work. For example, when they wanted to hold church services in Irish for the feast of St Patrick "he placed his church of St Alphonsus at the disposal of

[125] Quoted in Moffitt, M. ICM p 49

[126] Runaghan, P. Father Nugent's Liverpool. Birkenhead 2003. P 12

[127] Furnival, J. Children of the Second Spring . Gracewing 2005. P 114

[128] Ibid. Pp 269 & 270

the League" so that Irish-speaking priests like Fr McFadden of Gaoth Dobhar, Co. Donegal could preach there. [129]

The Irish poor in Liverpool, as in Ireland, were clearly adept at 'playing the field' when it came to dealing with the opposing Catholic/Protestant charitable endeavours. Pat O Mara (1901-1983) describes how his gang, because of hunger, regularly attended Cob Hall to obtain a free cob of bread at the end of the service which was designed to :"save the Irish Catholic slummy children from a life-long devotion to the Pope." They composed foul parodies of all the hymns and sang an insulting song about King Billy on their way home [130]

The Protestant poor could be similarly pragmatic : Gillespie describes how the Irish Christian Brothers set up a school in Sunderland, but found that the majority of very unruly children who swarmed into it were not Catholics. A local newspaper campaigned for a while about 250 Protestant boys being converted to the 'Popish religion' but when the brothers explained to the parents that they could not teach their children Protestant prayers the latter replied :"No matter...teach them what you please. I know you will teach them nothing but what is good." [131]

The Catholic Church in Liverpool seems to have had a similar tolerant attitude to the school set up in 1848 by Rev Abraham Hume in Gascoyne Street, which housed a number of Irish-speaking families. It was not far from Hodson Street where the priests 'rescued' poor Irish children from the ragged school set up by the proselytisers. Certainly Hume makes no mention of any Catholic opposition to the two free evening schools, which he says were in reality "Ragged Schools" This was probably because he adopted the non-confrontational approach of the Irish Society, which he refers to in his study. As mentioned earlier, the Catholic Church in Liverpool was clearly monitoring the work of those they regarded as proselytisers, like the ICM, and they appear to have extended this role to Ireland itself. When writing of John Yates, an English Catholic and Liberal city councillor who died in 1887 aged 80, Burke says :"He never trimmed his views on Catholic or Irish questions to gain applause, as witness his personal visit to Connemara to expose the Irish Church mission frauds..." [132] This is a reference to the exaggerated claims made by the ICM for the number of Catholics they had 'converted' in Conamara, particularly during the famine years when food was offered as an inducement. Many of these people switched back to Catholicism when the food crisis abated. The fact that Burke mentions the ICM in Conamara shows that he was aware of the organisation and its modus operandi. That both they and the IS had agents in Liverpool would undoubtedly have been of concern to him.

Coincidentally, John Yates was born in Haslingden and knew the Davitt family. He attended the opening of St Mary's Catholic Church in the town in 1859 and even called his home in Old Swan, Liverpool, 'Haslingden House.' When it was demolished in the 1960s to make way for a new housing development, the new street was called 'Haslingden Close', a lasting link between the two towns. Presumably, Yates would have learned something of the Irish language before embarking on his trip to Conamara, otherwise he would have found it difficult to "expose the Irish Church Mission frauds."

Did the efforts of the proselytisers to convert Irish-speaking Catholics endure in the longer term? The census of 1861 was the chief factor in exposing as false the ICM claims that many thousands of Catholics had converted. When the census results were revealed in May, 1863, they showed that, far from expanding due to Catholic conversions, the population of the Established Church actually fell by over 100,000 between 1834 and 1861, from 800,730 to 693,357. Clearly, many thousands of starving Catholics had converted temporarily in order to obtain the free food and clothing on offer from the ICM. When the famine finally ended in 1852 the 'jumpers' became Catholics again, especially following the mission campaigns organised by Bishops McHale and Cullen . [133]

DID THE LANGUAGE PASS TO THE SECOND GENERATION ?

We know from Canon Abraham Hume that the Auxiliary Irish Society was at work in the city, and thanks to his survey we have accurate statistics of the numbers of people who spoke Irish and where they lived.

[129] Murphy, B. Notes on the history of the Liverpool Gaelic League, 1939. unpublished

[130] O Mara, P. Autobiography of a Liverpool Slummy. P 62

[131] Gillespie, W. The Christian Brothers in England. Bristol 1975. P 66

[132] Burke, T. Catholic History of Liverpool. P 241

[133] Moffitt, M. ICM . p 124

To what extent did the language pass down to the second generation i.e. those Irish who were born and bred in Liverpool?

Most of the Irish people in his survey in Vauxhall were poor and had little education and as such did not leave much written evidence behind them in the form of diaries or biographies. That is not to say that they were not intelligent and did not understand what was going on around them. Just staying alive probably occupied most of their time. We are fortunate that one person, at least, from the area of the Hume survey did leave a written record, and a local historian, Michael Kelly has researched and written about his life.

James Carling (1857-1887) was born in Addison Street , the first street in the Hume survey of 1848. Addison Street had a total of 96 families, 29 of whom were Protestant. The total population of the street was 380. 30 of the 96 families are described as "Irish speaking". There were also 23 courts off Addison Street, containing 137 families, of whom 68 were Irish speaking. The 1861 census states that Henry Carling, father of James, was born in Hull and was 33 years of age, while his mother, Rose Carling, aged 33, was born in Ireland. James was the youngest of six children. Henry Carling, a blacking maker, moved around the country a fair bit as his eldest child, Catherine, aged 15, is listed as having been born in London, William (11) and John (9), in Hull, while Henry (7), Terence (5) and James (3) were all born in Liverpool. A married couple, Terence and Ann Jane Lynch (40) who were both born in Ireland are listed as living with the Carling family in 38 Addison Street "It is possible that Terence was the brother of Rose Carling." [134]

Frank Neal's book Black '47 makes clear that Irish people travelled all over the country looking for work, often meeting up with relatives and other Irish people in the areas in which they settled. So the Carlings would not be unusual in having lived in at least three different cities in Britain. We know also that Gaelic speakers linked up with other Gaelic speakers when they moved from city to city. (See later section on George and Richard Shorten.) Denis Gwynn mentions the large numbers of Irish speakers in ports like Liverpool and Cardiff in the West, and Hull and Newcastle in the East.[135]

The Carling brothers all went out on to the streets at an early age as pavement artists, and Kelly quotes from James writing as an adult : "Starved by a stepmother of a very unusual disposition, I sallied out into the world like Jack of the fairy tales to seek my fortune, and a living as well, at the ripe old age of five."[136]

He would not have been alone. Thomas Burke describes the efforts of Fr James Nugent to assist the many hundreds of poor Irish children who ended up begging or trading on the streets : " As early as 1849, he established, with the help of Mrs Baines, a house in Spitalfields, to feed and provide a bed for the poor waifs who had begun at that early age to infest the streets of Liverpool. They belonged entirely to the race from which the worthy priest himself had sprung, for the famine years made an impression on him which was never effaced." [137]. In the 1860s he opened a house in Soho Street "and on one night 647 wretched lads had been provided with a meal, and a makeshift arrangement had been made to provide 134 with a night's shelter." Bishop Goss said that there were 300 children running wild in the Holy Cross parish "neither attending school nor receiving adequate parental supervision."

Clearly, a knowledge of the English language was essential for these children if they were to survive on the streets by begging, peddling or working as pavement artists, even if the language they spoke at home might well have been Irish. Karen P. Corrigan discusses the pressure emigration put on the Irish language : "Thus migration launched a two-pronged attack on Gaelic: it significantly reduced the number of speakers and created a climate in which competence in English became a key to survival." Further on she states :"Languages which are perceived either as being low in status or as having marginal utilitarian value are rarely maintained." [138]

James Carling (8 years) was sentenced to six years in St George's Industrial School in 1865 after being apprehended by the police while working as a pavement artist. The school was run by Fr James Nugent and Carling was taught to read and write there. Upon release, aged 14, he was taken to Philadelphia by his older brother Henry. The two brothers managed to make a living through their art in the USA, and

---

[134] Kelly, M. Liverpool, the Irish Connection. Liverpool 2003. Pp 93-99

[135] Gwynn, D in Beck, G The English Catholics p 267

[136] Kelly, M. Liverpool the Irish Connection. Pp 93-99

[137] Burke, T. Catholic History of Liverpool. P 166

[138] Corrigan, K in the Irish in the new communities. (O Sullivan ed)

James was in regular contact by letter with his elder brother William who lived in Plymouth, Devon, where he was active in the Irish Home Rule movement. Michael Kelly has these letters and kindly shared them with me.

Carling is an Anglicised form of the Gaelic surname Ó Cairealláin and the Carlings claimed to be descended from the famous blind harper/composer Tarlach Ó Cairealláin (1670-1738). As O'Caireallain had seven children, this could well have been true. The family initially used the version O' Carolan and the first born child was registerd as William Carolan. One year later, John was registered as Carling. "I can only assume they changed their name to help them find work, as there was a lot of prejudice against Irish people." [139] Burke refers to this as the "No Irish need apply" maxim. James Carling was very proud of the connection and makes frequent references to it in his letters. He was clearly knowledgeable about Ó Cairealláin's life, for he refers to him as "the last of the bards" a name given to him by Oliver Goldsmith (1728-1774) who apparently met him when he was a child and wrote an account of him when he was an adult. Ó Cairealláin , although primarily a composer of music, did write poetry as well. This was all in Gaelic, as he had very little English. When his wife, Mary Maguire died, he wrote a beautiful poem in her honour containing these lines :

Fágadh 'na ndéidh sin liom féin mé go brónach

I ndeireadh mo shaoil's gan mo chéile bheith beo agam

Left after that alone and in sorrow

At the end of my life without my wife alive with me.

In a letter to his brother William, written in New York in 1883, James Carling says :"It is a mistake to suppose that Turlough Caroling (Goldsmith's 'Carolan the Blind') was in reality the last of the Irish bards." He goes on to state that his descendants, born on English soil, carried on the tradition of composing songs and tunes and mentions his own father in particular. James obviously learnt some Gaelic songs from him, but as he could not write the language, he uses the English phonetic system when quoting titles or words. In a letter written in New York in 1884 James Carling asks of William "Did I send you these two lines from Ta me ma codlas na duze me : Tau may ma culls, tau may ma culls, Tau may ma culls, na doozy may."

When first reading this I immediately recognised these as lines from the old Gaelic song Táimse im chodladh and sent Michael Kelly the words. Seán O Sé, the popular Gaelic singer from Cork, and a frequent visitor to Liverpool over the years, included this song in his CD An Poc ar Buile in 2010 (Gael Linn) . Michael then sent me an undated A4 page with a long poem on it entitled "Ta me ma codlas, Na duze me; or, I'm asleep and don't waken me. " The poem is largely in English and is signed 'James Carling, The Bard. At the bottom it states : J.White, Printer, 8 Rose-place, Scotland Road, Liverpool. Here we have written evidence that a second generation Irish person, who was born in Vauxhall just 9 years after Abraham Hume did his survey there, maintained an interest in the Gaelic language and culture. The people who were dismissed as "bipeds, old and young, holding converse in a jargon that would be difficult to interpret" (The Picturesque Handbook to Liverpool, 1842) were actually the custodians of one of the most ancient languages and cultures in Europe.

James Carling returned to Liverpool in 1887, apparently to collect as many of his father's songs and ballads as he could. Unfortunately he became ill and died the same year and was buried in a paupers grave in Walton Cemetery. Carling is now recognised in the USA as being a hugely talented artist. His entries into a competition to provide the illustrations for Edgar Allen Poe's special gift edition of his poem The Raven in 1883 are displayed at the Poe Shrine in Richmond, Virginia. James Carling's talent is also recognised in his home town. An annual 'street art' competition named after him is organised in the city. The James Carling Gallery operates in Bold Street, and when a new public house was opened in 2002 on Walton Vale, near to where he is buried, it was named The Raven in his honour and contains a display

---

[139] Kelly, M. Private discussion, November 2012

about his life and copies of his artwork. The latter initiative came about at the suggestion of the Walton Local History Group. The fact that someone born into poverty in Liverpool's 'Irish ghetto' was able to find an outlet for his artistic talents is a source of great pride to the local Irish community. I write here as a Liverpool-Irish person born in Walton Hospital, close to Carling's grave.

I would argue that the fact that Carling clearly remembered at least part of the song Táimse im chodladh (see appendix) which is quite revolutionary in its sentiments, is strong evidence that Gaelic was an important part of the culture of the Irish community in Liverpool, even though the language was of no economic benefit to them.

(When the Independent Report on the Hillsborough Disaster was released in Liverpool on September 12, 2012 a vigil was held outside St George's Hall in the city centre and Terry Coyne, a member of the local branch of Comhaltas Ceolteoirí Éireann played Táimse im Chodladh in front of the thousands of people in attendance.Incidentally, when the Chieftens visited New York after 9:11, they played Táimse im Chodladh at the site of the World Trade Centre.)

James Carling was just one example of the thousands of hugely talented Irish children who began their lives as beggars on the streets of Liverpool. It was clearly heartbreaking for Fr Nugent to witness this and he commented that he met more gifted and talented children among the Irish poor in Liverpool than one would ever meet among "the young aristocrats or 'nobs' of Eton, Harrow and Rugby" but their talents were never to have the opportunity to flower.[140]

AU UNEASY RELATIONSHIP – THE IRISH LANGUAGE AND THE CHURCH AFTER THE FAMINE.

The immediate post-famine period left the Catholic Church in a difficult, and contradictory situation with regard to the use of the Irish language both in church, and amongst Catholics. In the first place, over a million people had fled abroad and settled in countries which were overwhelmingly Protestant. It was feared that these people were in grave danger of losing their faith, not to mention enduring intense poverty and often death.

Secondly, the Protestant 'soupers' had shown the impact they could have in winning over converts by using the Irish language to teach the poor and by offering food as an inducement to convert. Although the figures produced by the ICM were subsequently proved to be wildly exaggerated, and many of the 'converts' reverted back to Catholicism once the worst of the famine was over, the tactics of the ICM produced something of a backlash against the language on the part of many of the clergy in Ireland, which lasted for some years. This development encouraged them to use the 'food for souls' tactic :"Catholic activists realised that the most effective answer to Protestant missionary activity was the distribution of food and clothing, the provision of free schooling and the establishment of alternative Catholic facilities for destitute children in areas of extreme poverty."[141] The various projects established by Father Nugent in Liverpool can be seen in that context.

Unfortunately for the Catholic church, they still did not possess enough priests to meet the needs of their flock, particularly Irish-speaking priests who would be able to win back the souls lost in strongly Irish-speaking areas like Conamara and/or travel to Britain, America and Australia to attend to the thousands of monoglot Irish speakers who had left in the wake of the famine. Maynooth was still an English-speaking institution, and so were most of its graduate priests. O Céirin states that the census of 1851 indicated that there were about 200 students and staff at the college who had registered themselves as Irish-speakers; at most only 45%. [142]

Not all students at Maynooth were happy in the well-to-do, Anglo-centric atmosphere there; some wished to break away and work amongst the poorer sections of society, which were overwhelmingly Irish-speaking. The layman Edmund Rice (1762-1844) had set a precedent when he founded a school to teach the poor in Waterford in 1802 from which sprang the Irish Christian Brothers order, which received papal recognition in 1820. As mentioned earlier, the Christian Brothers were great champions of the Irish language and they produced a grammar text for the language which was eventually used in most schools in Ireland.

In 1832 four trainee priests, James Lynch, Peter Kenrick, Anthony Reynolds and Michael Burke, left

---

[140] Bennett, Canon. Father Nugent. Liverpool 1949. P 31

[141] Moffitt . ICM p 115

[142] ibid p 178

Maynooth and set up a community house in Ushers Quay, Dublin, where they ran a school. They were attracted by the philosophy and teachings of St Vincent De Paul (1581-1660). From this small group sprang the modern-day Irish Vincentians whose fluency in Irish was to prove vital in winning back many Catholics lost to the soupers in Conamara. They were given the use of the chapel of St Peters in Phibsboro, Dublin and eventually set up a seminary in Castleknock, on the outskirts of the city. It is interesting to note that this happened around the same time as the Church of Ireland had set up St Columba's College in Dublin, which promoted the teaching of Irish for those training for the priesthood.

Another Maynooth student was to join them in 1835 : John Hand (1807-1846). He came from a peasant background and as a child had been evicted along with his parents from their little farm in Oldcastle, County Meath. He witnessed the large-scale emigration which was taking place prior to the famine and saw that there was a need to train Irish-speaking priests like himself to follow the emigrants. He worked tirelessly to raise the funds to set up All Hallows College, Drumcondra, Dublin, which opened in 1842, just three years before the start of the Famine and the mass emigration that went with it. John Hand died of TB in 1846, but the first graduates from the seminary he set up were to prove essential in ministering to the famine refugees in English-speaking countries, many of whom spoke only Irish.

As pointed out earlier, Bishop Brown of Liverpool was reluctant to recruit Irish priests prior to the famine. However, after ten priests died during the fever epidemics in the city, he wrote to All Hallows College in Dublin "begging for some Irish priests" [143] but had little luck as Australia and America were competing for them. Corrigan states that there is substantial evidence that clerics sent to minister to migrants in America were chosen not just on the basis of their 'good constitution' but also because they could 'speak Irish.' "Thus the Rev Andrew Talty, in a letter to Dr Woodcock of All Hallows College, Dublin, claims that this is why he was selected. Furthermore, when describing the nature of his parishioners in Virginia he claims that 'the Irish won't think anything (of any person) unless they know Irish." The letter was dated 1851.

This was also the case in Britain, where Irish-speaking priests followed the migrants when they dispersed from Liverpool throughout the country. Father Thomas Martin from Castletown Co. Meath was sent to St Mary's Catholic Church, Haslingden, where he ministered from 1854 to 1880. He was succeeded by Fr Michael Dillon from Clara, Co. Offaly, who ministered from 1880 to 1895. Both men were Irish speakers. "Unless a priest could speak Irish he could not administer confession." The priests also heard confessions from Irish speakers in nearby towns like Blackburn and Accrington. [144]

With regard to the English Midlands, John Denvir states :"It will be remembered how Father Sherlock was sent to minister to the Irish in Bilston, one of these Black Country towns, because he could hear their confessions in their native tongue." [145] Denvir quotes from A.M. Sullivan, who visited the district in 1856 as a special correspondent for the Irish Nation. Most of them, he found, still talked Irish constantly and of Wednesbury he wrote that "in very many of the houses not one of the women could speak English, and I doubt that in a single house Irish was not the prevalent language."

As we have seen from the Hume survey, many parts of Liverpool were like Wednesbury. However, whereas the Irish Protestant Rev Abraham Hume had a positive, pro-active, non-judgemental attitude to the language, and even commenced to learn the language himself, the English Catholic Bishop Brown appeared to despise the Irish and their language. When he died in 1856 he was replaced by another Lancashire Catholic with even more reactionary views than himself- Alexander Goss (1814-1872)

Goss was born in Ormskirk, a market town some 20 miles north of Liverpool. Irish farm labourers and harvesters had been travelling to the town for many years prior to the famine and a few hundred had settled there. The famine caused the Irish population of the town to increase so that by 1851 it was about 1,197 out of a total population of 6,000 i.e. 20% [146] The church of St Anne's was opened in 1850 to cope with the huge increase in the size of the town's Catholic population and is still in operation.

Alexander Goss was bishop from 1856 till his death in 1872 and was responsible for providing priests and churches for the newly arrived Irish. As he was "intensely English" and a staunch monarchist, he had no interest whatsoever in their linguistic and cultural needs. Cardinal Wiseman reported to Rome that Goss was always telling his people :"I am English, I am a real John Bull, indeed I am a Lancashire man." Like

[143] Doyle. Op cit p 78

[144] Private discussion with Dr John Dunleavy 12/11/12

[145] Denvir, J . Irish in Britain p 418

[146] Bradshaw, PE. A Study of Ormskirk, mid 19th Century, based on 1851 census. 1979. Ormskirk Library, Lancs

his predecessor, Bishop Brown, Goss was reluctant to employ Irish priests. He made this clear in a letter to Dean Greenhalgh of Chorley in 1856. "On one occasion he went so far as to claim that he had no Irish priests in his diocese, for it was an English diocese ruled by an English Bishop, and the clergy who served it were English, whatever their country of origin."[147]

He was, of course, only too well aware that large numbers of Catholics in his diocese were not English and could not speak that language. Accordingly, in 1856, he moved Fr. Gerald O' Reilly (brother of the later bishop) from the Isle of Man to Our Lady's, Eldon Street, Liverpool , "where his knowledge of Gaelic would be invaluable."[148] However, in 1861 when Pierse Power, the parish priest of St Anthony's on nearby Scotland Road asked permission to recruit another Irish-speaking priest, like himself, directly from Ireland, Goss refused, and offered him instead the services of a priest from Belgium, Fr Van Hee.(1831-1894).

Another Irish-speaking priest was needed at St Anthony's in order to assist Pierse Power in hearing the confessions of the parishioners (Catholics were obliged to go to confession at least once a year) and to visit the sick. No doubt Fr Van Hee found this out when he arrived on Scotland Road, and being from mainland Europe, he probably would not have had the narrow, Anglo-centric outlook of the bishops Brown and Goss. He might well have adopted the strategy of the Italian priest Father Signini in South Wales, who compiled for his own use a small conversation book in Irish, so that he could hear confessions. Van Hee was from the Flemish part of Belgium, not far from Leuven where the oldest Catholic University in the world, founded in 1425, is situated. The Irish Franciscans established their college in Leuven in 1607 and its impressive gate-way still carries the message : "Do chun Glóire Dé agus Ónóra na hÉireann "- for the glory of God and the honour of Ireland." (the dedication in the Annals of the Four Masters).[149] I do not know if Van Hee studied Irish at Leuven, but as he moved to Our Lady's Eldon Street in 1864, where he was on the rota for the Liverpool Workhouse, a knowledge of the language would have been essential for his work.

Reference has already been made to Fr Luigi Gentili who reported to Rome prior to the famine about the lack of interest shown by George Brown in the Irish communities in Lancashire. It is interesting to contrast the respect shown by priests from the continent for the Irish Catholics with the disdain shown towards them by some members of the English hierarchy. Irish Catholicism would have enjoyed a respect amongst European clergy, who were aware of the Irish role in the revival of Christianity in Europe in earlier centuries. Numerous European churches named in honour of Irish saints are testament to this. Additionally, they would have recognised that the bulk of the Irish population had remained committed to the Catholic faith during and after the Reformation, despite persecution by a Protestant English monarchy.

To Catholics from multi-lingual mainland Europe, it was perfectly natural that Catholics from Ireland would have their own language and might not necessarily speak that of neighbouring England. But many English people appeared to equate a lack of knowledge of their language with ignorance. Goss justified his lack of interest in his Irish-speaking flock by arguing that they were not the only group with special needs. He had recently (1861) sent two of his students to train in Germany so that the spiritual needs of 'the many German immigrants ' could be met.[150] The neglect of the needs of Irish-speaking Catholics in Liverpool had the same result as it had in Ireland : reduced participation in formal religious practice. In 1865, only 43% of Catholics in Liverpool attended mass regularly.[151]

The negative attitude of some English Catholics towards their Irish counterparts is well-documented as the quotations from Doyle above illustrate. William Gillespie says of the English Catholics :"They were embarrassed by the arrival of so many Catholic Irish who had so obviously little love of the British constitution or government. How could the respectable English Catholics rejoice to have their ranks swollen by immigrants who would clearly lower the whole social tone of the faith?"[152]

Bishop George Beck's book contains two essays with quotations from Barbara Charlton, an upper class

[147] Doyle. Op cit. Pp 45-46

[148] Doyle. Op cit. P 77

[149] www.leuveninstitute.eu

[150] Doyle Op cit. p 77

[151] O Siadhail, P. An Béaslaíoch. Dublin 2007. P 21

[152] ibid p 3

Catholic lady, which bear out Gillespie's view. In 1860, at a house party at the Marquis of Westminster's, some embarrassment was caused when disparaging references were made to Roman Catholics. The Marquis intervened, mentioning she was a "Roman Catholic lady" and Mrs Charlton retorted :"Yes, but an English Catholic, not an Irish one, which is all the difference in the world. English Catholics are responsible beings who are taught right from wrong, whereas Irish Catholics, belonging to a yet savage nation, know no better and are perhaps excusable on that account."[153] Needless to say, she had little time for Irish priests either and summed up her view of people from that country thus :"All Irish, all dirty, and helpless.....and unworthy objects." Charlton was from Northumbria, where Aidan and a group of Irish monks travelling from Iona, had arrived in 635 CE to bring Christianity, and literacy, to that part of England, establishing a monastery at Lindisfarne.

POLITICISATION OF THE USE OF IRISH

The relationship between the English Catholics and the Irish Catholics is something of a paradox, to say the least. We have already seen that several English priests gave their lives attending to the mainly Irish victims of the fever of 1847 in Liverpool. John Denvir states that Canon Fisher, the Vicar General of the diocese, was very anti-Irish and tried to prevent anyone connected with the Catholic Times (a pro-home Rule newspaper owned by Fr Nugent and edited by Denvir) from coming into contact with Bishop Goss, whom Denvir describes as " a typical Englishman of the best kind.".[154] He goes on to praise Goss's sermons. Apparently the bishop was very hard-working and confidently and stridently stood up for the rights of Catholics in a country which was still by and large hostile to his faith. His first official act as Bishop of Liverpool was the laying of the foundation stone of the new church of St Vincent de Paul on James Street, which took place on the transferred feast of St Patrick, 1856 . He used the occasion to praise the Irish residents of the parish "We have no fears, because we are satisfied you carry with you the faith which you have inherited from your fathers," he told them. He later attended the usual dinner in honour of St Patrick's Day, organised by the city's Catholic Club. [155]

It would appear that, whatever their politics, the most important thing to both Goss and Denvir was their Catholicism. Denvir, who was a member of the Irish Republican organisation the Fenian Brotherhood and who was totally supportive of the Irish language and culture, praised Goss because he was a formidable defender and advocate of the Catholic faith. Goss, a staunch English monarchist who had no time at all for the Fenians or the Irish language and culture, was willing to praise and defend Irish Catholics because they were Catholic.

From a cultural and linguistic standpoint, it is important to remind ourselves of the Irish Protestant Abraham Hume (1814-1884). Like Denvir (1834-1916) he was born in Ulster, and was also clearly interested in the Irish language. Like Goss, he was a monarchist and supporter of the British establishment. Denvir makes no mention of Abraham Hume in his two books about the Irish in Britain and yet he praises Goss. Many Irish-speaking Catholics did not have such a contradictory position : they welcomed the efforts of organisations like the Irish Society in teaching them to read and write in their own language and in their other charitable work and were not particularly bothered that they were Protestants. (see earlier section on P.T. McGinley) The fact that they were fellow Irish speakers was the most important thing. They had more in common with them than they had with Anglo-centric English Catholics like Bishop Goss, who despised their language and culture. If Alexander Goss had reached out to the thousands of Irish people in Liverpool and learnt Irish the way Abraham Hume did, and had promoted the language in the way the Welsh dissenters promoted their language via their chapels in Liverpool, then the story of the Irish language in the city might well have been very different. 'Leakage' to proselytisers might well have been reduced.

Doyle defends Goss, saying : "It is clear that he felt that it was only by playing down their nationality that the Irish could be fully accepted in English society.."[156]

Following what was described by a contemporary Irish poet as "the odious extermination of 1847"[157] there was a large degree of sympathy among the Irish community in Britain for the revolutionary Irish

[153] Beck . op cit pp 142 & 269-70

[154] Denvir- Life Story.. Op cit p 156

[155] Burke, T. Op cit pp 126-127

[156] ibid p 46

[157] Póirtéir, P (ed) Gnéithe an Ghorta, Dublin 1995. P 98

Confederation which sought an independent Irish republic. Edward Kenealy (1819-80), for example, the Irish-speaking lawyer, was heavily involved in the London Irish Confederation. According to his daughter he intended to go to Ireland to take part in the 1848 rising but was dissuaded by a friend. The Irish Confederation had been set up in January 1847 by the Young Ireland group when they broke away from O'Connell's moderate Repeal Association. The Confederation was led by William Smith O'Brien, a Protestant landowner, MP and Irish-language enthusiast who was convinced that the suffering of the famine justified armed revolt.

Irish-speaking doctors in Liverpool had witnessed first-hand the horrors of the epidemics and starvation in the city and a number were prominent in the Irish Confederates. Their number included Francis O' Donnell and Patrick Murphy. A cousin of Murphy, Terence Bellew McManus, was the leader of the movement in Liverpool. He travelled to Ireland to take part in the rising at Ballingarry, Co. Tipperary in July 1848. Not surprisingly, the large-scale support for the Republicans in Liverpool further encouraged the anti-Irish outlook of Bishop Brown and that of Bishop Goss, who succeeded him in 1856.

Bishop Goss was also very hostile to the later Irish Republican group the Fenians. He famously forbade the Liverpool Irish from attending a planned procession in honour of the executed Manchester Martyrs in 1867 and claimed "that the Fenian movement had been begun by Irishmen who were opposed to the Catholic Church."[158] He even suspected the Catholic Young Men's Society (CYMS) of being a possible republican front.[159] The Fenian Brotherhood had been formed in America in 1858 to assist the Irish Republican Brotherhood (IRB) which had been founded in Dublin on St Patrick's Day of that year with the aim of overthrowing British rule in Ireland and establishing a republic. The word 'Fenian' was used to describe both groups. The name, adapted from the legendary Fianna warriors, had been chosen by John O'Mahony (1819-1877), the Irish scholar and linguist, and deliberately linked the aspiration for an independent republic with the ancient Gaelic culture. As such it provided yet another reason, if one was needed, for hostility towards the Irish language on the part of the British establishment and sections of the Catholic hierarchy. Typical of its leaders was Diarmaid (Jeremiah) O'Donovan Rossa (1831-1915) whose ill-treatment, along with that of Michael Davitt, while imprisoned in England, aroused international concern.

O'Donovan Rossa, as a young man, had put his name in Irish over his shop in Bandon, Co. Cork to encourage his customers to use the Irish language in their business with him. This was in itself an act of political defiance, as the anti-Irish legislation of the time stated that all business names had to be stated in English only. As Thomas Davis (1814-1845) argued before the famine, this legislation made the Irish language both a cultural and a political issue (see page 52)

O'Donovan Rossa taught Irish for a time at the Mechanics Institute in Dublin. A horrified Cardinal Paul Cullen discovered that some of his clergy were attending these classes and he hurriedly slapped a ban on them. [160] O'Donovan Rossa visited Liverpool in 1906 where he was given a tremendous welcome when he delivered a lecture in the Picton Hall. O'Donovan Rossa was a close family friend of John O'Donovan and his family. Some of John's sons took the Fenian oath from O'Donovan Rossa . Edmond, the second son, worked as a Fenian organiser in Connacht with O'Donovan Rossa and Mark Ryan, the Irish-speaking refugee who passed through Liverpool in 1860(see earlier section). Mark Ryan said of O'Donovan Rossa : "All his life he spoke the Irish language with fluency and pleasure, and ardently advocated its revival."[161] John O' Donovan's youngest son Richard, also a Fenian, moved to Liverpool in 1875 and spent his working life in the city. O'Donovan Rossa's visit in 1906 would have provided the men with the opportunity to renew their acquaintance. In 1881 the very name "O'Donovan Rossa" caused alarm in Liverpool as the Lord Mayor, William B. Forwood, (1840-1928) blamed him and his Fenian comrades in America for organising the failed attempt to blow up the town hall in June of that year. The discovery of one of O Donovan Rosa's billheads rolled up in the mechanism of an "infernal machine" had caused panic in Liverpool police barracks when William Forwood had pulled out the piece of paper and accidentally started the mechanism.[162]

---

[158] Burke, T. Op cit. 180-81

[159] Doyle. Op cit p 42

[160] O Céirin, Op cit. P 178. Seán O Lúing queries this.

[161] Ryan, M. Op cit p 89

[162] Forwood, WB. Recollections of a Busy Life 1840 -1910. Liverpool 1911

Despite the dislike of Brown and Goss for Irish culture and politics, they had to tolerate it to some extent, such was the strength of the Irish community in Liverpool. As already mentioned, Bishop Goss moved an Irish-speaking priest to Our Lady's, Eldon Street, Vauxhall in 1856, but refused permission for the employment of an Irish-speaking priest at St Anthony's on Scotland Road. Such double-dealing with regard to the Irish language also seems to have been happening in Ireland . The Catholic Church mounted a vigorous campaign to win back those who been 'converted' by the ICM during the Famine years (1845-52). Irish-speaking Vincentian priests were sent to areas badly affected by the proselytisers, such as Irish-speaking districts like Conamara and the Dingle area of Kerry. Others were sent to Dublin, where the predominant language was English but where Irish was widely spoken amongst the poor, in districts such as the Coombe. If no Irish-speaking priests were available, then Irish Christian Brothers were used to interpret the message of the Church, which was simply that converts should return to the Catholic Church, or be damned to hell.

There was also a vigorous campaign of ostracism and persecution of ICM converts and mission staff . People were socially isolated, insulted and at times physically attacked. Catholic priests particularly warned against Irish-speaking Bible readers and text teachers (like the mother of PT MacGinley mentioned earlier). "Bless yourselves when you meet them. Don't have anything to do with them,"[163] they told their flock. The same thing seems to have happened in Liverpool : when describing the 'rescue' of poor Famine migrants from the proselytisers by Catholic priests, Burke quotes one of the insulting songs heard in Ireland about converts "damning their sowls for penny rowls, and flitches of hairy bacon." [164]He also describes a seven year old child calling one of his piers " a turncoat and a Protestant. "

Figure 1. This painting by David Jacques, which can be seen in the Newz bar in Liverpool, carries the title of the Gaelic League newspaper - An Claidheamh Solas - which was sold in Liverpool.

[163] Moffitt op cit. p 123

[164] Burke, op cit p 108

An tSnaidm.

An céad gníom.

Radarc : Oifig Seagáin Uí Dranagáin.

Bord i lár an urláir, cataoir mór ar a cúlaid agus cataoireacha eile gac taob de. Fuinneog ra cúl agus dorar ar an láim deir ag déanam irteac ar an oifig móir. Deagán acair ó'n dorar ro teine geal. Tá páipéaraí agus leabra ar an mbord. Mórán purdaí a bainear le gnó oifige rgapta ar fuaid an treompa. Tá Labrár Ó Liatáin i n-a ruide go rocair ruaimnearac i gcataoir ar agaid na teinead, a cora rinte ar clár an trimléir agur é ag féacaint go dlút ar coramlact (pótograp) mná óige. I gcionn tamaillín árouigeann ré an coramlact cun a béil. Cuireann garúr na hoifige a ceann irteac ra dorar. Tar éir beit ag féacaint ar Labrár, readann ré port mear. Preabann an fear óg i n-a fearam go capaid, agur cuireann an coramlact i n-a póca.

Labrár.—Tá go mait, a buacaill.

> [Imtigeann an garúr. Tornuigeann an t-ógánac ar páipéaraí do tógáil ar an mála tá ar an urlár le n-a air. Seagán Ó Dranagáin irteac.]

An Dranagánac.—Hum! Tá tú ar air arír, a Labráir.

Labrár (ag cur caoi ar na páipéaraíb agur ag labairt go naerac).—Táim, a taoirig.

An D.—Sead, bí na laeteanca raoire go mait agat tall, ir dóca.

Labrár.—Go han-mait. Díor ag obair i gcomnuide.

An D.—Cionnur do caitin Roinn na hEorpa leat?

Labrár.—Ní'l aon cúir gearáin agam i n-a taod. Ir fearr liom beit ar air ra baile, ám, (ag déanam gotaí) mar deir an file——

An D. (go géar).—Stad an fiadantar rain; tá coinne agam le cuairt duine uaraíl.

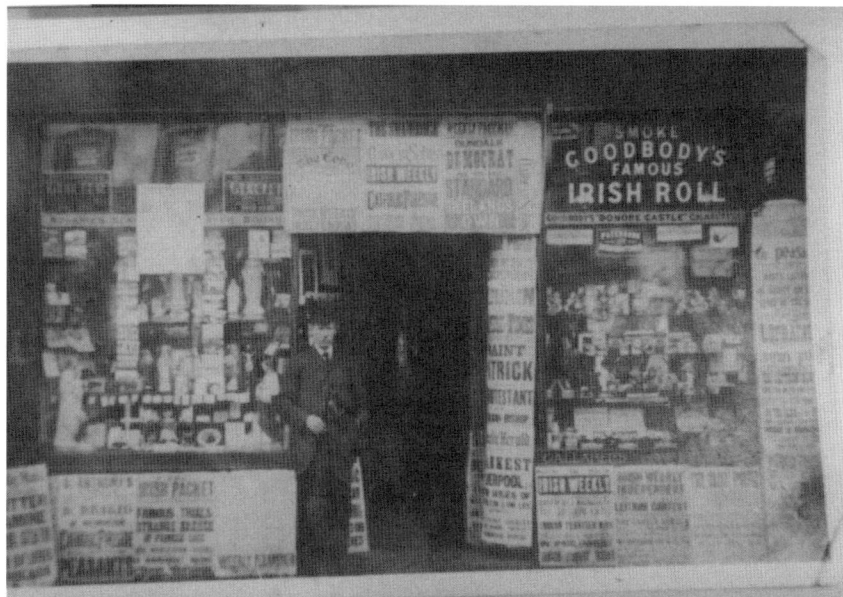

Figure 3: Peter Murphy, outside his '98 shop, Scotland Place, Liverpool, circa 1909. Above the door, is an advert for the Gaelic League newspaper, 'An Claidheamh Solas.' Peter and his son Brian – mentioned in the text – were both in the Gaelic League.

All this seems to have had a negative impact on the Irish language in areas of Ireland where people were bilingual. There was clearly no point in the clergy railing against the Irish language in areas where people were monoglot speakers of that language, but in places like Allt an Iarainn, Co. Donegal, the home-place of PT MacGinely, the Catholic clergy seems to have put pressure on people to abandon the Irish language in favour of English.

"The teaching and reading of Irish in those areas where proselytism was vigorous was forbidden, collections of manuscripts were made and burnt publicly and preachers fulminated against the language from the pulpit," says O Céirin.[165] This was happening at the time that the Church of Ireland minister, Rev JH Todd (1805-1869), was busy purchasing and preserving priceless Irish manuscripts in Trinity College along with John O'Donovan (1806-1861) and his brother-in-law Eoin O'Curry . Canon Coslett Ó Cuinn (Quinn) (1907-1995) who attended the College of St Columba in Dublin (where he noted the witty inscription :'Moladh gach anáil an Tiarna'- praise every breath of the Lord -on the organ) says of that period :"Priests forbade people to read Irish Bibles and held bonfires of them and other books and manuscripts. To be able to read Irish was rather a dangerous sign of Protestant inclinations!"[166]

THE IRISH LANGUAGE IN LIVERPOOL AFTER THE FAMINE

Given the situation with regard to the Catholic Church and the Irish language in Ireland, it is perhaps not surprising that the proudly-English Bishop Goss felt able to ignore and obstruct the language and culture of the Irish community in Liverpool by, for example, refusing to appoint Irish-speaking priests in areas where they were clearly needed. Many of his clergy, such as Fr James Nugent, were more sympathetic to the cultural needs of the Irish in the city. Alcohol abuse was a major problem in the community and in 1872 Nugent established the Total Abstinence League of the Cross, which was heavily influenced by the

---

[165] ibid pp 177-8

[166] In Mistéil (ed) Op cit. p 29

47

temperance movement of the Irish-speaking priest Fr Mathew of Cork. He came to Liverpool in 1843, 1849 and again in 1854, when the two men met . In 1875 Fr Nugent built the League of the Cross Hall, off St Anne Street. The Hall could seat 2,000 people and was an alternative to public houses. There were ten branches of the League in Liverpool and the central one - the Fr Mathew branch - was based in the League Hall. With the help of the Fenian John Denvir, Nugent put on Irish musical entertainment and short plays which were very popular with the local poor, although Goss condemned Nugent for encouraging a dangerous sense of nationality.

Irish-speakers clearly felt comfortable in the League Hall. When Fr Nugent returned there after a lengthy recuperative absence in 1888, his supporters hung out a banner which read :"Cead mille failthe, saggarth aroon", which the Catholic Times newspaper described as an "appropriate motto."[167] This was written decades before the spelling of Irish was standardised, at a time when very few speakers of the language were literate in it (the schools in Britain and Ireland only taught people how to read and write in English). In modern Irish it would read :"Céad míle fáilte, a shagairt, a rún," or in English : "One hundred thousand welcomes, dear priest." This appears to be adapted from a famous Irish song, Eibhlín a Rún, composed by Cearbhall O' Dalaigh in 1386. The chorus contains the words : Céad míle fáilte romhat, Eibhlín a rún."

This is significant for a number of reasons. It shows that members of the Irish community in Liverpool had pride in their ancient culture, a culture which they had brought with them from Ireland. Despite the extreme poverty they experienced, with death all around them, they held on to it and were keen to display it openly. Songs were a medium by which the language, or at least bits of it, could be passed down through the generations in a largely English-speaking city.

Father James Nugent (1822-1924) was born in Hunter Street, off Byrom Street, Liverpool, the son of John Nugent, who had emigrated from his home in County Meath in Ireland and was almost certainly an Irish-speaker. At least one other member of John's family, his sister Catherine, also came from Ireland to live in Liverpool. Nugent's mother, Mary Rice, was from Lancashire and was a convert from the Anglican Church. Nugent was clearly liked and respected by the local Irish community, who joined his League of the Cross organisation, and ensured it was a financial success. Presumably they would not have gone to the trouble of making a large banner, written in Irish, to hang from the gallery of the hall as a welcome unless they knew that James Nugent would understand what it meant and would like the fact that they were communicating their sentiments in Irish. They were clearly proud of their language and were willing to use it on a public occasion to express their affection for a popular member of their community. Some of them were at least partially literate in the language, despite the fact that, up until 1878, it was not taught in Irish schools at all, and many young children were beaten if they dared speak the language within ear-shot of a teacher.

John Denvir (1834-1916), the Fenian who worked for Fr Nugent's Catholic Times newspaper and organised the entertainment in the League Hall, was born in County Down, but moved to Liverpool as a small child with his parents. His first language was English, but he was very aware and proud of the use of Irish in Liverpool. He was a supporter of the Gaelic League/Conradh na Gaeilge (founded in 1893) and his book Life Story of an Old Rebel is interspersed with Gaelic words and phrases, written in English phonetics. He was great friends with Mark Ryan, the Irish-speaking doctor who had passed through Liverpool as a famine refugee from Galway and who returned to the city as a Fenian agent.

Denvir tells of an aunt of his (a sister of his mother's) who could speak the Ulster dialect of Irish fluently. When she married a man called Hughey Roney they ran a public house together in Crosbie Street, in the south end of Liverpool. According to Denvir's account, all the local residents were from the West of Ireland and spoke nothing but Irish amongst themselves. Through the course of her business she "acquired the Connaught Irish and accent," [168] This was before 1844, the year Fr Mathew delivered the total abstinence pledge in Irish to thousands of people in Liverpool. Denvir says that when Hugh Roney retired the pub was carried on by his daughter and her husband, the Ulster man John McArdle " a good, decent patriotic Irishman." This was the pub which later lost so much business due to Fr Mathew's temperance crusade that it had to start selling groceries.

Thomas Burke, the Irish Nationalist city councillor and author of Catholic History of Liverpool, was from a Conamara family and lived in Blundell Street, parallel to Crosbie Street. The tradition of Irish-speaking people coming to this part of Liverpool continued on into the 20th century. Tommy Walsh (1930-2010) was

[167] Catholic Times 29 June 1888. In Belchem, op cit, p 226

[168] Denvir, Life Story p 15

born in Blundell Street and his father, Colum, came to England from Carraroe,(in Conamara) Co. Galway in 1922. "My father was a native Irish speaker, who would have spoken little or no English until he came to England. He thought in Irish and prayed in Irish until he died at almost 99 years of age." Tommy makes the point that this was not even the most Irish part of the city :"I was to learn later in life that Scotland Road, on the north side, was the Irish side of town." [169]

Irish-speaking priests were clearly a vital part of the community in Liverpool in the 19th century, despite the English-nationalist views of Bishop Goss. Thomas Burke argued :" The common link of nationality enabled priests and people to work much more harmoniously than was possible with clergy of English birth or training..."[170]

John Denvir describes the work of one on the Irish-speaking priests in Liverpool, around 1875 : Father Peter McGrath " a dear old Soggarth at St Joseph's." He had worked with Denvir's uncle, Father Bernard O'Loughlin, in the Isle of Man, where the locals had been able to understand him when he spoke Gaelic with them. "Before I met Father McGrath in Liverpool I had heard from my uncle of his delightful and saintly character. He was a ministering angel among our people in his district, which was one of the poorest in Liverpool. His charity was unbounded. Going on a sick call and being at the end of his monetary resources- for let his friends give him ever so much he would never leave himself a penny- he had been known to give away his own underclothing, and even to carry away his bed-clothes to relieve some cases of abject poverty."[171]

When writing about Father McGrath, Denvir makes the point that the Gaelic spoken on the Isle of Man and that spoken in the Scottish Highlands and in Ireland were very similar. He makes the same point later in the book when he describes his business in Liverpool printing a Scottish Gaelic Prayer Book for Father Campbell, one of the Jesuit priests in the city. The prayer book was for use among the Catholic congregations in the Highlands and Islands of Scotland and Denvir gave copies to Irish-speaking friends like John Rogers and Timothy MacSweeny :"and they both could read the Scottish Gaelic easily, showing, of course, how closely the Irish and Scottish Gaels were, with the Manx, united in one branch of the Celtic race, as distinguished from the Bretons and the Welsh."[172]

In conclusion, such was the strength of the Irish-speaking community in Liverpool after the famine that Catholic clergy who could speak the language were essential and contemporary commentators like John Denvir noted their dedication to their parishioners. Second-generation Irishman James Nugent was also cognizant of the cultural, as well as the spiritual, needs of this community. However, the stridently English nationalist views of Bishop Goss, which were reinforced by the activities of the Fenians, meant that the Irish-speaking Catholic community were tolerated, rather than assisted or encouraged by the church hierarchy.

THE DECLINE OF IRISH

A complex combination of social, economic and political factors have been instrumental in the decline of the Irish language from Norman times to the present day. The attitude of officialdom has played an important part throughout. From the on-set of colonisation through to the twentieth century, there was an enduring and systematic policy of suppression of the Irish language in public life, especially in business and commerce, the legal system, government administration and education.

The census of 1851 showed that 80% of people in large parts of the west still spoke Irish, but in other areas the figures indicated that the language was in retreat. Robert McAdam, the Belfast industrialist, doubted the accuracy of the figures: "It is well known that in various districts where the two languages co-exist, but where English now predominates, numbers of individuals returned themselves as ignorant of the Irish language either from a sort of false shame or from a secret dream that the Government in making this enquiry (for the first time) had some concealed motive, which could not be for their good."[173]

The continued decline in the use of the Irish language is shown by each subsequent ten year census from 1861. "The 1871 census came to the stark conclusion that 'within relatively few years' Irish would cease

[169] Walsh, T. Being Irish in Liverpool.Liverpool 2011. P p 11 & 23

[170] ibid 236-237

[171] Denvir, Life Story pp 186-188

[172] ibid 259

[173] O Snodaigh op cit p 26

to exist.'" [174] One wonders if there was an element of wishful thinking in the above statement, given that government policy had always been geared towards eradicating the language. As early as 1366 the Irish Parliament, which was dominated by Norman invaders, passed the Statutes of Kilkenny which banned the use of the Irish language, customs and dress by English and loyal Irish subjects. As the indigenous inhabitants of the country were gradually deprived of their land, particularly after the so-called 'plantations' begun under the Tudors, their language was increasingly marginalised. By 1641 59% of the land was still in the hands of native population, but following the Cromwellian land settlement and subsequent Penal Laws, this had fallen to 5 per cent by 1778.

What this represents is the displacement of the indigenous, Gaelic-speaking chieftains and the Catholic Anglo-Irish aristocracy (who had adopted Gaelic ways) by a new class of English landowners who despised the local culture and people but who needed them as manual labour on their estates. Arthur Young, in 1776, describes how the indigenous inhabitants still regarded the land as belonging to them : " a gentleman's labourer, upon his death, leaves his masters estate to his son."[175]

The Irish language had no standing in law and all legal business was conducted through English. As the President of Ireland recently pointed out in a lecture about the Irish in Liverpool : "The eviction notices which were pinned to their cottages in Ireland were always written in English, a language most of them did not understand." [176] This was also noted by pro-democracy campaigner John Mitchel (1815-1875), the son of a Presbyterian clergyman, who ran a law practice in Banbridge, Co. Down. He visited Galway in 1847 to assess the impact of the Famine and noted that those who could not speak English were in an especially vulnerable position when it came to eviction.[177]

Seán de Fréine argues that the destruction of the social system (education, arts, law, medicine, literature and commerce) that used Gaelic was an important cause of the demise of the language. Allied to this was the contempt the new landowners felt, and showed, towards the native population. "chuaigh an uirisleacht go smior sna Gaeil. Níorbh í an bhoctaineacht ba mheasa de, ach an tarcaisne a leanadh !" which translates as, 'This humiliation was felt deeply by the Gaelic people. It was not the poverty that was the worst thing, but the contempt that went with it."[178]

THE STATUS OF THE IRISH LANGUAGE IN THE PRESENT DAY

The Administration of Courts (Ireland) Act of 1737 forbade the use of the Irish language in courts of law. This Act, which is still in force, has been the subject of legal challenges by Irish language speakers in Northern Ireland. "Is there a law against speaking Irish in the street?" one Irish speaker asked in Belfast Magistrates Court in May 1984.[179] He had been charged with obstructing an RUC constable by giving his name in Irish when stopped in the street. He refused to speak English when he appeared in court. A man in Co. Roscommon was charged with the same offence when he gave his name in Irish to an RIC constable in 1900.[180]

Irish speakers argued that the 1737 Act was incompatible with the European Charter for Regional and Minority Language (which the UK has signed) and was in breach of the European Convention on Human Rights. However this was dismissed by the High Court in Belfast in July 2009 and by the Court of Appeal in June 2010.

Mark Durkan, leader of the SDLP, raised the issue in the Northern Ireland Assembly in April 2010, when he asked the Justice Minister, David Ford (Alliance Party) if it might be possible to repeal the Act. "The Act to which the member refers is the subject of legal proceedings," was the reply.[181]

When I raised the issue with the NI Department of Justice, I was informed in a statement (19/4/2013)

[174] Quoted in Feasta March 2008 p. 9

[175] Young, A. Tour of Ireland (1) London 1776. P 170

[176] O Higgins, M. D. Address at Institute of Irish Studies, Liverpool 21/11/12

[177] Mitchel, J. The Last Conquest of Ireland. 1861

[178] In Póirtéir, P. Gnéithe an Ghorta. P 65

[179] Guardian newspaper 22/5/1984

[180] O Fearail, P. Op cit p 22

[181] see www.legislation.gov.uk

:"The 1737 Act provides that the language of the courts is English, and languages other than English are not permitted in court, except where a party to proceedings cannot speak or does not understand English. Policy on the Irish language generally is a matter for agreement by the Executive as a whole. Arising from the St Andrews Agreement, there is a statutory duty of the Northern Ireland Executive to adopt a strategy for the entrenchment and protection of the Irish language. The Minister of Justice has stated that he will consider the issue of the use of the Irish language in courts in the context of this strategy, although a draft strategy has not yet been considered by the Executive."

So, no change there yet.

Fr Peadar O' Laoghaire makes the point that anyone who could not speak and/or understand English in Ireland was at a serious disadvantage and was vulnerable to exploitation :"For example, in any kind of legal affair, the man with English was able to turn black into white on them and they had no means of defending themselves. If they gave their account in Gaelic, none would understand them- except, perhaps, the man who was planning to do them an injustice."[182]

In nineteenth century Ireland this policy could have fatal consequences, as in the celebrated case of Maolra Seoighe, who was tried in 1883 for his alleged part in the murder of a family of five by a gang near Mám Trasna on the Mayo/Galway border. The Irish Nationalist MP Timothy Harrington described the case to Parliament in August 1883 :"He was conveyed more than 200 miles from his home, and put on trial in Dublin. Not a single word of English was he able to speak; not a single word of his own language were the jury who tried him able to comprehend..."[183]

The jury took just six minutes to find Seoighe guilty. The judge, who also did not speak Irish, sentenced him to death. Two others who were found guilty with him wrote a statement before their execution saying that Seoighe had nothing to do with the murder. The governor of Galway prison informed the Lord Lieutenant of Ireland, Earl Spencer of this. He sent a telegram back saying :"The law must take its course." James Joyce wrote an article (one of a series of nine) about the case for his local newspaper when living in Trieste.[184] Davitt denounced the obvious injustice, and such was the anger it caused, Parnell formed the Maamtrasna Alliance with the Tories and brought down Gladstone's Liberal Government in 1885.

Liverpool-born (1951) David Alton, who was made a Life Peer in 1997 after serving for nearly 20 years as a Liberal/Lib-Dem MP in the city, heard the story of Maolra Seoighe from his Mayo-born mother, an Irish-speaker from Tuar Mhic Éadaigh, which is near Mám Trasna. He is behind a campaign in Parliament to persuade the authorities to review the case of Seoighe and " to declare him the victim of a miscarriage of justice and to concede that he was falsely convicted and executed." (www.davidalton.net). Alton spoke at a commemoration in Galway to mark the 130th anniversary of the execution in December 2012, alongside Johnny Joyce, a descendant of Maolra Seoighe.

Irish-speakers who found themselves before the courts in England would likewise find little sympathy for their lack of understanding of English, as described by Finnegan in a case in York, a town where there were many Irish speakers. When one of them found himself in court, his attempt to speak, and comprehend, English was at first mocked by the magistrate "for the court's amusement" and then angrily condemned .[185]

Under British administration all official business had to be conducted in English. As already noted, O' Donovan Rossa broke the law by putting up his name - ' Diarmaid Ó Donnabháin Rosa' – in Irish on a sign outside his shop in Cork. [186] When registering births and deaths, in school or in court, an English equivalent – often something which simply sounded similar to the Irish (such as Jeremiah instead of Diarmaid) - had to be used. Maolra Seoighe was named as Myles Joyce in court. My mother, Síle Ní Dhálaigh (1915-1976) was registered at birth in Co. Meath as Julia Daly.

---

[182] My Story (trans) Op Cit p 148

[183] Quoted in Beo, No. 140 Nollaig 2012 article by Breandán Delap. www.beo.ie

[184] Joyce, J. Il Piccolo della Sera (Trieste) 16/9/07 Ireland at the Bar.

[185] Finnegan, F. Poverty & Prejudice: A Study of Irish Immigrants in York. Cork 1982 p 174

[186] Corkery, D, The Fortunes of the Irish Language. Cork 1954. P 121

ORIGINS OF THE REVIVAL MOVEMENT

This state of affairs was often challenged by pro-democracy campaigners in Ireland. Cork-born Thomas Davis (1814-1845), the son of a Protestant army-surgeon father, was co-founder of The Nation newspaper along with his friends John Blake Dillon and Charles Gavan Duffy. They were all members of Daniel O'Connell's Repeal Association, who later became known as Young Ireland.

Unlike O'Connell, however, Davis, championed the cause of the Irish language in his writings in The Nation. He described as "politic cruelty" the passing of Acts such as that of Edward IV which compelled Irish people to give up their Gaelic names in favour of English ones, and Henry VIII's Act for English Order, Habitat and Language 1537 which compelled them to use English speech. :"To lose your native tongue, and learn that of an alien, is the worst badge of conquest- it is the chain on the soul," Davis argued. He recognised the importance of the Irish language in the struggle for political freedom :"A people without a language of its own is only half a nation. A nation should guard its language more than its territories - 'tis a surer barrier, and more important frontier, than fortress or river." He argued that the language should be taught to all, rich and poor alike.[187]

These essays of Thomas Davis are recognised as the beginning of the modern revival movements and they had a huge impact, particularly in places like Liverpool where so many Irish speakers had emigrated. Given the low rates of literacy and income at the time, public house owners would commonly buy and read out The Nation for the benefit of their customers. John Denvir describes listening to such readings on Sunday evenings in John McArdle's public house in the strongly Irish-speaking Crosbie Street area, along with the owners son, who was so moved by what he heard that he ended up becoming a journalist and working on The Nation.[188]

Wall [189]argues that the fact that pro-democracy papers like The Nation were all written in English was a factor in the decline of the language, and there is a certain irony in a publican in Liverpool reading out articles in English about the importance of the Irish language to a largely Irish-speaking audience. But at least Davis (a lawyer) was drawing their attention to the inherently undemocratic nature of the anti-Irish language legislation which was in force and helped to instil pride in a language which was mocked by journals like Punch. Furthermore, Davis opposed the narrow Catholic perspective of O'Connell, and thus helped to promote the language to all.

Although Davis died at the early age of 31 in 1845, his support for the Irish language was continued by The Nation newspaper. Ulick Burke (1829-1887), a young student at Maynooth, wrote a series of simple Irish lessons for the paper which proved to be very popular, both with learners of the language and also people who were fluent in it, though illiterate, a result of the policy of forbidding the language in the National schools.

LANGUAGE REVIVAL AND THE IRISH IN BRITAIN

We know that these lessons were popular with the Irish community in England, including one James Ronan, a wholesale tea and coffee merchant in Salford, Manchester. He had arrived in Liverpool during the famine years (around 1849) and had managed to do well in business. He never lost his interest in his native language, however ."Ba mhór an chúis mí-shásaimh dó nach raibh deis ag lucht labhartha na Gaeilge eolas ceart a chur ar an teanga; eolas a chuirfeadh ar a gcumas í a labhairt go cruinn agus go foirfe." (It was a great source of dissatisfaction to him that Irish speakers did not have the chance to learn the correct way to use the language; knowledge to enable them to speak the language with perfection) [190]. What is now called An Caighdeán Oifigiúil (The Official Standard) did not exist at the time and so pronunciation, spelling, use of grammar etc could differ widely, particularly between speakers of the language from different parts of Ireland. When they emigrated and met up with people from other parts of Ireland there was a chance for disagreement about the way Irish was spoken and written, if they happened to be literate in it.

Ronan hoped that the situation would improve when Ulick Burke's Easy Lessons were published in the Nation, but he was disappointed that nobody in Ireland continued on the good work of the priest. He expressed his feelings in a long letter to Seán Mag Flainn (dated 28/6/1869) in which he said that it was more than 10 years since the Easy Lessons had come out and nothing had happened in the interim. He

---

[187] Davis, T. Our National Language pp158-165 Essays on Ireland. Scott Library. London

[188] Denvir, Life Story p 15

[189] Wall, M. Decline of the Irish Language in O Cuív ibid p 81

[190] Ní Mhuiríosa, M. Réamh Chonraitheoiri Dublin 1968 p 25-26.

said that he had knowledge of self-instructional courses in other European languages and he wished to put this knowledge to use in the cause of the Irish language.

He then wrote to Canon Ulick Burke in Tuam, who replied that he was more than happy to assist James Ronan in his project in Salford, the production of The Keltic Journal and Educator. Ronan, who paid for the whole project out of his own pocket, used to send the proofs for the magazine across the Irish Sea for Canon Burke to check, causing considerable delays. Despite all the difficulties, the Salford Irish language publication ran for nine editions between 1869 and 1871. The fact that the first journal of the Irish language revival was published and printed in Lancashire is further proof of the extent of the distinctive linguistic heritage of the Irish community in Britain.

Further proof comes from James Ronan's suggestion that an organisation be formed to promote the Irish language. He suggested that Archbishop MacHale should be the president, and his cousin Canon Ulick Burke the professor. He sent Burke a long list of names of people in England who would be willing to support the project. His suggestion was taken up in 1876. The Society for the Preservation of the Irish Language (SPIL) was founded in Dublin, with MacHale as its patron. It encouraged people who knew the language to speak it, and those who did not to learn it. To help with the latter aim Canon Ulick Burke updated his Easy Lessons. These were published in a series of three cheap books 1877-1879.

Much of this activity was financed out of the pocket of the Church of Ireland clergyman, Rev Maxwell H. Close (1822-1903). He apparently started to learn Irish while a geology student in Connacht and continued his interest in the language after he was ordained and went to work in Leicester and the midlands 1848-61. He joined SPIL at its foundation and was a keen advocate of bilingualism in Ireland[191]

To assist those who could already speak the language, SPIL aimed to produce a Modern Irish Literature. This was a major deficiency at the time : people who were making individual efforts to promote the language were severely hampered by the lack of books available in Irish. For example, when Fr Peadar O' Laoghaire set up a small night school where he was working in the village of Kilworth, Co. Cork in 1867; "There was no book in Gaelic to be had in any place at that time- unless a person procured the Foreign Bible, but you couldn't have anything to do with that because of the bad name the Soupers had left it."[192] As soon as he heard of the formation of SPIL he wrote to them and ordered books for teaching a beginners class he had started in Rathcormack.

Another aim of SPIL was :"To procure that the Irish language shall be taught in the Schools of Ireland, especially in the Irish-speaking districts." [193]This was a direct challenge to the state, as the British government did not recognise the existence of Irish. SPIL quickly won the support of Home Rule MPs like Isaac Butt and with his help they successfully petitioned parliament to allow Irish to be taught as an 'additional subject' in schools in Ireland in 1878. The petition was signed by many Protestant and Catholic clergymen, including Archbishop MacHale.

This was a very minor concession on the part of the state, as all it meant was that Irish could be taught as an optional subject outside normal school hours- primary pupils would have to stay behind at the end of the school day to learn to read and write Irish (if they already spoke it) or learn it from scratch if they did not. All this depended, of course, on there being a teacher willing and able to do this. No extra resources were made available to teach Irish, and English was to remain the language of instruction in the National Schools, as it had been since their inception in 1831. However, at least there was a reduction in the brutality associated with the policy : "In fact, the most important result of this recognition was that it brought about the abolition of the screeen and the floggings for speaking Irish." [194]Under the screeen, or 'bata scór' system, primary school pupils had to wear a stick around their necks; every time the child spoke Irish, a notch was carved on the stick, and at the end of the day the child was punished – frequently through corporal punishment - for each offence.

The British authorities still insisted that the children be registered for school in the Anglicised version of their names, even though family and friends used the original Gaelic form. This persisted right up to the Anglo-Irish Treaty of 1921. Dorothy Harrison-Therman examined the registers in the school house on Tory Island. Co. Donegal, which covered the years 1874 to the 1980s. She notes that up to 1921

[191] Ní Mhuiriosa. Op cit p 53

[192] My Story . Op cit p 96

[193] Ní Mhuiríosa. Op cit p 6

[194] Green, D in O Tuama , S (ed) The Gaelic League Idea. Mercia Press 1972 p 17

Maighréad Ní Dhuibhir was registered as 'Margaret Diver', Pádraig O Dubhagáin as 'Patrick Duggan' etc. [195]

By 1888 Irish was being taught in only 51 National Schools in the whole country. The situation improved slightly as the Irish language movement gathered pace but in 1903 the Gaelic League/Conradh na Gaeilge issued the following advice on the matter :"The teaching of Irish as an 'extra' subject is no longer confined to the fifth and sixth classes, but may be extended to any class capable of receiving instruction in the subject."[196] It would appear to have taken a quarter of a century (1878-1903) for the Irish language concession granted to SPIL to be extended to the whole school; a good indicator of official hostility to the policy.

In 1992 Bríd Bn Uí Chuinneagán (1912-2008) described to me (in Irish) her first day at Meenacross National School in Gleann Cholm Cille, Co. Donegal, where she still lived. She and her friends were very excited as they walked down the lane together as they had heard that all the lessons in school were in English, a language they themselves did not speak. She was not bitter about this. She just accepted it that that was the way things were. She could still remember some of the books that were used in school, such as The Kings and Queens of England and The Life and Times of Horatio Nelson and was keen to discuss them with me, in English.

Presumably such texts were used throughout the British Empire. Pat O' Mara (1901-1983) attended St Peter's School in Seel Street, Liverpool, which was filled mainly with Irish-Catholic boys. "But the tutors in this school, though all of them were Catholic, had been trained in England and all their teaching smacked of this English training. The Empire and the sacredness of its preservation ran through every text book like a leitmotif." [197]

The influence of the Society for the Preservation of the Irish Language spread to all the major Irish centres in Britain. PT McGinley (1857-1942) who had attempted to learn to read Irish as a youth from the Bedell Bible, first came across SPIL, not in Ireland, but in the north of England :"I first came across one of their centres in Leeds, and hailed it as an oasis in the Anglo-Saxon desert."[198]

In order to promote the teaching of Irish in national schools, a Special Literary Prize Fund was initiated in 1882 by Birmingham-based Dr Alan Boyd Simpson. This distributed prize money for Gaelic essays. Its patron was Rev. Dr Croke, the Vice-president Rev M.H Close (mentioned above). It also enjoyed the support of the Rev Euseby Cleaver (Romford, England) and Rev James Stevenson, Co. Cork. Rev. Euseby Cleaver was the most generous benefactor: in 1892 , when he was living in Dolgelly, North Wales, he provided prizes for schools in seven Irish counties, from Cork up to Donegal. Although a Protestant, Cleaver paid for the publication of a new edition of St Patrick's Prayer Book by Father Nolan. "A thousand copies of the issue are to be distributed free among the National Schools, Christian Brothers' Schools and convent schools in Irish-speaking districts"[199]

Another of the aims of SPIL was to publish a bilingual journal, something that had already been done in Salford 1869-1871. It is another indicator of the strength of the Irish language among the emigrant community abroad that the second such journal was launched not in Ireland, but in the USA, where there were a number of societies organised for the sole purpose of promoting Irish culture. Some of these societies held regular classes in conversational modern Irish. One is reminded here of the words of O' Tuathaigh quoted near the start of this book :" the emigrant-ship bound for Boston or Liverpool usually had a heavy quota of Irish speakers aboard."

In October 1881 the first edition of An Gaodhal was published in New York. It was founded by Micheál Ó Lócháin from Galway. He remained editor until his death in 1899. This bilingual monthly continued publication until 1903 and later editions contained work by W.B. Yeats, Lady Gregory and Synge, as well as illustrations by Jack B. Yeats. By that stage it was more commonly known as The Gael. [200]

The material in Irish came from both Ireland and the USA, with readers from various states sending in

[195] Harrison-Therman, D. Stories from Tory Island. Dublin 1989

[196] O Suilleabháin, D. An Piarsach agus Conradh na Gaeilge. Dublin 1980 p 182

[197] O Mara Op cit p 56

[198] Fitzgerald, WG. Op cit p 447

[199] Ní Mhuiríosa . Op cit p 64

[200] Ní Mhuiríosa. Op cit p 24

songs and poems they remembered from home or had copied down from older members of the community. Some people sent in poems they had copied from ancient manuscripts that they had brought with them across the Atlantic- a clear indication of the great love and respect they had for their native language despite years of official repression.

An Irish language journal appeared in Ireland in 1882 : the Gaelic Journal/Irisleabhar na Gaedhilge. It was founded by former members of SPIL who broke away to form the Gaelic Union. It contained articles in both Irish and English as well as material to help learners. We know that it was sold and read in Liverpool as the Central Library still has copies. In a letter to the editor - Eoin Mac Neill - in 1890, P.L. Beasley, father of Piaras Béaslaí (1881-1965) says that all the members of his family admired the magazine greatly, and Piaras (aged 15) "almost idolises it." "He finds it invaluable as he is studying Irish by himself."[201]

CHANGES IN THE OUTLOOK OF THE CATHOLIC CHURCH

The references above to the priests Ulick Burke (An Canónach Uileog de Búrca) (1829- 1887) and Peadar O' Laoghaire (1839- 1920) make it clear that the climate as regards the Irish language became more favourable within the Catholic Church in the second half of the nineteenth century. This was not the result of any major policy change, but appears to have been the result of the efforts of various individuals who were sympathetic towards the language. But there were still those who were hostile and obstructive, with the result that at times the policy of the Church could appear to be contradictory. For example, when the Irish-speaking clergy in England were invited to a meeting in support of the teaching of Irish in schools in April 1878 in the Westminster Palace Hotel London (organised by SPIL) – a meeting attended by Isaac Butt and other Irish MPs - none of them attended or sent their apologies, in spite of the support of Archbishop McHale for the initiative. [202]

The 1861 census revealed that the claims of the ICM regarding the number of conversions it had made were false, and the organisation lost momentum, especially after 1870. This helped reduce the fears some Catholic clergy had about the Irish language being a vehicle for proselytisers. They consequently became more favourably disposed towards it.

As already mentioned, the census figures for 1851 indicate that there were about 200 students and staff at Maynooth College who registered themselves as Irish speakers. When Peadar O' Laoghaire attended - 1861-1867 - the figure would have been much lower. Having grown up in rural Cork, he had assumed that everyone in Ireland could speak Irish. When he went to Maynooth he met people who did not have a word of the language, (or claimed not to) which amazed him. Despite the negativity about the language, particularly during the time of the Fenians, he persisted with it and taught it to others when he became a priest. This was to have a direct bearing on Liverpool as the Irish language group he started in Macroom, Co. Cork, soon after the formation of SPIL, was a great success and was called Cumann na nGael (The Gaelic Society). So much so that in 1905 Macroom could still be described as 'the most Gaelic town in Co. Cork.' [203] When George Shorten emigrated to Liverpool from Cork in 1898 the Cumann Gaelach presented him with an inscribed book, which is still in the possession of the Liverpool branch of Conradh na Gaeilge/The Gaelic League. He was a key activist in this organisation in both Liverpool and Glasgow, while his brother Richard did similar work in London.

Another factor behind the change in the Catholic Church's attitude to the language was the failure of Fenian Rising of 1867. Church leaders like Cardinal Cullen and Bishop Moriarty had condemned the Fenians, but many of the clergy opposed the execution of the Manchester Martyrs in 1867 and supported the amnesty movement for Fenian prisoners. Peadar O' Laoghaire describes the impact of this event on himself and his colleagues and names one of the chapters in his book: ' A Dhia, saor Éire' after the slogan shouted by the condemned men. (God save Ireland) This is the slogan on the Fenian monument in Liverpool's Ford Cemetery.

This book, published in 1915 in the old script, was widely read in Liverpool as evidenced by the copies still held by older members of the Irish community. One of Fr Ulick Burke's initiatives was the proposal to abandon the old script in order to make the written language more accessible and easier and cheaper to print. Unfortunately his suggestion was not acted upon, although the Free State Government began to

---

[201] O Siadhail, P Op cit p 34

[202] Ni Mhuiriosa Op cit p 7

[203] O Céirin . Op cit p 107

use Roman script for its official publications in the 1920s. Irish schools persisted with the old script up to the 1960s and older members of the Gaelic League in Liverpool were still writing in it in the 1990s.

In 1882 Eugene O'Growny (1863-1899) formed an Irish Society in Maynooth College. Despite official apathy towards Irish (in 1887 the Scholastic Council actually put to a vote whether Irish should be continued to be taught at Maynooth, and decided it would be, but only as an optional subject [204]) O'Growny continued to promote the language there until his ordination in 1889 and was a regular contributor to the Gaelic Journal. He was made editor of that magazine in 1891 and appointed Professor of Irish at Maynooth the same year. In 1892 he befriended SPIL activist Douglas Hyde (1860-1949) and gave him a tour of Maynooth. O'Growney told him that about 200 students (40% of the current enrolment) had some knowledge of Irish. [205]O'Growney went on to produce the best-selling series of three books called Simple Lessons in Irish, copies of which still abound in Liverpool. Furthermore, priests arriving in the city from Maynooth were generally more sympathetic towards the language than had been the case previously. This was even more important than ever after 1879, when, in spite of the Land Campaign led by Michael Davitt and Parnell, a fresh round of evictions led to an upsurge in emigration and a further decline in the number of Irish speakers.

In conclusion, the decline of the Fenian movement, changes in attitude amongst the hierarchy and at Maynooth, led to a softening in the Catholic Church's attitude towards the Irish language in the latter half of the nineteenth century. As the revival movement gained strength, the attitude of the Catholic Church towards the Irish language became more sympathetic.

THE IRISH REVIVAL IN LIVERPOOL

Irish emigrants arriving in Liverpool in the second half of the nineteenth century would have been well-aware of the low status of their native language in Ireland in matters of the law, education and general social advancement and presumably would have expected similar attitudes in England. Karen Corrigan argues that this was the case in the USA:" Thus, while Gaelic enclaves are reported to have existed in several states- especially in the urban tenements of the eastern seaboard- such speakers were under considerable pressure from their peers and from the xenophobic attitudes of the community at large to cast off the low-status language with which they were afflicted."[206]

Fortunately for the Irish arriving in Liverpool, there were factors which aided the use of their language. As already noted, Fr James Nugent's League Hall, founded in 1874, regularly provided Irish entertainment and Irish speakers clearly felt comfortable there. In addition, Archbishop Goss had died suddenly in 1872. His successor was the Irish-speaking Bernard O'Reilly (1824-1894). He had served as curate of St Patrick's and parish priest at St Vincent's. He had managed to persuade the Irish Christian Brothers to remain at the school there until 1876 following their decision to leave the city in protest at the inspections and supervision introduced by the 1870 Education Act. "To the Irish population their departure was a serious loss, as they inculcated love of country as well as of religion, and wielded an extraordinary influence over the children of the Irish race."[207] (Thomas Whiteside, who succeeded O'Reilly in 1894, persuaded the Christian Brothers to return to Liverpool).

Bernard O Reilly's brother, Fr Gerald O'Reilly, had served at Our Lady's, Eldon Street, where his knowledge of Irish was "invaluable." [208] Bishop O'Reilly obviously had a much more positive attitude to Irish priests, and Irish things generally, than his predecessors Brown and Goss. In his report to the Vatican in December 1887 he stated that there were 235 secular priests working in the diocese (ie priests who were not members of a particular order such as the Vincentians) and of these, 93 were 'foreign' , of which 81 were Irish (plus 10 Belgians and two Germans). 55 of the Irish priests were permanently attached to the diocese, while the 26 others were on temporary loan for set periods from dioceses in Ireland. [209] This meant that Irish-speaking Catholics had a far better chance of practising their religion through Irish. This is borne out by the bilingual weekly newspaper Fáinne an Lae, first published in 1898. In an article entitled 'The National Church and the National language,' William O'Brien stated that

[204] Corish, PJ. Maynooth College 1795-1995 p.213

[205] Dunleavy J&G Douglas Hyde. California 1991. P 179

[206] ibid p 154

[207] Burke, T, Catholic History of Liverpool. P 192

[208] Doyle Op cit p 77

[209] Doyle Op cit. p 78

though he had many times been to mass in Irish-speaking areas the only times he had heard a sermon in Irish was in a church in Liverpool. Note he says "times", so presumably it was a regular event. [210] It is probable that he was referring to the sermons of Fr Pierse Power, who was parish priest at St Anthony's 1859-68 and later served at St John's, Kirkdale, until his death in 1895. His nephew, Fr Patrick O'Donovan (1834-1915) also preached in Irish at St Brigid's, Bevington Bush, off Scotland Road.

Irish speakers also had the services on at least two Irish-speaking doctors: brothers Alexander Murray Bligh (1833-1922) and John Bligh (1840-1913). Like the Irish-speaking, London-based doctors Mark and Paddy Ryan, the Bligh brothers were from Co. Galway, and like the Ryan brothers, they were prominent members of the Gaelic League. The Blighs maintained practices in the city centre and the north end Irish area. The fact that Irish speakers there could discuss their medical problems in their own language with a sympathetic person might well have been a huge encouragement to ordinary people to use Irish. This was certainly the case with Dr Mark Ryan, down in London, who "was always delighted to have a chat with an Irish speaker, no matter how humble his position. Londoners were often surprised to see a well-dressed man and a roughly-clad coal-porter engaged in a most animated conversation in a strange language, which seemed full of humour and to shatter social distinctions." [211] Dr John Bligh in particular took a special interest in ancient Irish manuscripts, particularly those relating to medicine. He was described thus in 1893: "Dr Bligh was a great student of the Irish language and literature. The subject is especially interesting, because Gaelic is one of the still living Celtic languages. Dr Bligh chats with the ardour of an enthusiast on this, to him, attractive theme." [212]

The Bligh brothers were not the only educated Irish people in Liverpool who were taking an interest in the language : in 1884 John Denvir (1834-1916) had launched the Irish Literary Institute, which changed its name to The Liverpool Irish Literary Society in 1893. This society organised lectures in Irish history and literature as well as poetry sessions and "founded (I write subject to correction) what I believe was the first Irish language class started in Great Britain..." [213] Journalists, including some from Fr Nugent's Catholic Times newspaper, were the biggest occupational group in the Institute and LILS. Liam P. O' Riain (Liam Ryan), assistant editor of Catholic Times, wrote, in 1894 :

"Certain Liverpool Irishmen have striven with great zeal during the past decade to accomplish a revival of Celtic ideas amongst their brethren and neighbours. Theirs is a most creditable record, telling of perseverance through depressing days. Liverpool or Lancashire generally cannot be called particularly literary, but most of the area is exceptionally interesting to the student of Irish thoughts and manners. Great novels are yet to be written of Irish life in Lancashire. Another Douglas Hyde might find within it as much Gaelic wealth to gather up as at home in the wild ways of Connaught." [214]

These were prophetic words, as Liverpool did indeed, within the next few years, produce a number of outstanding writers in the Irish language, whose enthusiasm impressed many people, including Tolstoy ! A further factor encouraging the Irish language movement in Liverpool was the appointment, in 1883, of Kuno Meyer (1858-1919) as a lecturer in German. His application was supported by John Rhys, Professor of Celtic in Oxford, who described him as "an excellent and most promising Celtic Scholar," [215] indicating that Kuno Meyer was a leading light in the Celtic-Irish scholarly movement. That movement, in alliance with the Gaelic League/Conradh na Gaeilge and the corresponding literary movement expressing itself in English - of which W.B. Yeats and Lady Augusta Gregory were representative - was one of three streams which flowed side by side. Meyer quickly introduced Celtic studies to Liverpool University, taking classes in Welsh and Irish. He was appointed Reader in that subject in 1902.

The fact that Celtic scholars from mainland Europe, like Meyer, Graziadio Ascoli, Johann Kaspar Zeuss, Heinrich Zimmer and Ernst Windisch were proclaiming the importance of the Irish language in the context of European civilization, gave great confidence to the Irish language movement and helped to stifle the opposition of those academics who deemed it not worthy of study.

An Irish scholar, Dr Douglas Hyde (1860-1949) was very much on the same wavelength as these

---

[210] O Fearail Op cit p 7

[211] Fenian Memories - editor's introduction

[212] Orchard, BG. Liverpool's Legion of Honour. Birkenhead 1893 (quoted in Kelly M. Liverpool's Irish connection)

[213] O Siadhail op cit p 32

[214] O Siadhail op cit 32

[215] O Lúing, S. Kuno Meyer Dublin 1991. P 3

continental scholars. Born in Co. Sligo, the son of a Church of Ireland minister, he gained a Doctorate of Laws at Trinity College and then devoted himself to writing and lecturing on Irish literature. He had joined The Society for the Preservation of the Irish Language when he was 17, after learning to speak the language in Co. Roscommon, where his father had been appointed Rector of Tibohine in 1867.

The lecture Hyde delivered to the National Literary Society in Dublin in November 1892, entitled 'The Necessity for De-Anglicising Ireland' was to provide the impetus for the formation of the Gaelic League/Conradh na Gaeilge the following year. 1893 was also the year he married Lucy Komentina Kurtz in St Nicholas' Church of England, Blundell Sands, Merseyside, and signed the register in Irish. A plaque was unveiled in that church on October 10, 1993, by the Liverpool branch of the Gaelic League, exactly 100 years since the day of the wedding.

The non-sectarian nature of the Gaelic League helped to attract support. The group's first vice-president was the Rev. Euseby Cleaver (1826-1894), mentioned earlier. He was replaced, upon his death by Fr Eugene O' Growney. It was probably as a result of Gaelic League activities that the percentage of Irish-speakers recorded in the census in the north of Ireland rose from 1.3% in 1891 to 2.3% in 1911. Protestant ministers were prominent in the movement there.[216]

The Liverpool branch of the Gaelic League was founded in 1896, before many large towns in Ireland had a branch of the organisation, indicating that there was a groundswell of interest and support for the language in the city. Prior to its formation, Irish classes were taught by Michael Lowe, originally from the west of Ireland. Michael is described as a small, aged man, who "fired with enthusiasm all who knew him." [217] The incentive to form a branch of the Gaelic League in the city may have come from a lecture on the Irish language given to the Liverpool Irish Literary Society in March 1896 by Fr. Risteard de Hindeberg (Richard Henbry 1863-1916) He was from an Irish-speaking family in Waterford, and after ordination at All Hallows in 1892 he moved to Salford. He was for a time chaplain in Whittington work house near Manchester. Such places usually had a number of Irish-speaking inmates, particularly amongst the elderly, so Fr Hindeberg's presence would have been most valuable.

The John O' Donovan branch of the Gaelic League was registered on May 1st 1896. It was named after the great Irish scholar mentioned earlier in this book. His son, Richard (1848-1939), a Fenian, came to live in Liverpool in 1875 and worked for many years for the Royal Insurance Company. He attended Kuno Meyer's classes in middle Irish in 1884. He eventually retired to Prestatyn. The branch was also known as the Edge Hill Branch, as that was Michael Lowe's home area. He was a parishioner at St Anne's Overbury Street. He taught two classes at the school of St Nicholas' Pro-cathedral, Copperas Hill, (bombed out in the war, and now the site of the GPO sorting office). This arrangement came about because of the sympathetic attitude of the administrator, Fr Alphonse Maurus, a Belgian. Dr John Bligh was president of the branch.

THE IRISH LANGUAGE AMONGST THE SECOND GENERATION IN LIVERPOOL

Although it is likely that many second generation Irish on Merseyside spoke Irish at home, it was primarily the Gaelic League which promoted cultural and social activities through the medium of Irish. By the early twentieth century, the League had a number of thriving branches on Merseyside. The Edge Hill branch, which soon became known simply as the Liverpool branch of the Gaelic League, published their own text-book The Principles of Irish Reading, which was written by 'ML', presumably Michael Lowe [218]. Learners had difficulty with the ancient Gaelic script. As already mentioned, this is not very easy to read, and some activists like Canon Ulick Burke advocated its abandonment in favour of ordinary Roman script. This branch appeared to attract a lot of people who were trying to learn the language, rather than those who could already speak it. The native speakers mainly lived in the north end. The League grew rapidly in this district. Native speaker Martin Grealy organised the Kirkdale branch in 1897. The Bootle branch was registered in January 1900 while the Archbishop McHale branch was founded in October of that year in Scotland Road. The Father O' Growney branch was founded at St Mary's Highfield Street in March 1903. This would indicate that there were viable Irish-speaking communities in the north end prior to the First World War. There was activity in other parts of Merseyside as well : Irish classes, taught by the Rev. Fr. Carton,[219] were started in autumn 1897 in the Birkenhead Irish Club, while Gaelic League branches were

[216] O Snodaigh Op cit pp 28-29

[217] Murphy, B. Op cit

[218] The Gaelic Journal November 1898

[219] Gaelic Journal November 1897

started in Rock Ferry and Old Swan (1903).

Amongst second generation Irish - those born to Irish families and living in Irish communities in the region – there was a strong community of Irish speakers. The achievements of prominent members of this community demonstrated the breadth of Irish language culture in the region, and the extent of interest in it. Here I will briefly examine the life and work of five of their number : Norma Borthwick, Piras Béaslaí, Alphonsus Ó Labhradha , Cesca Trench and Gerard Patrick O'Loughlin.

The first Oireachtas Irish Festival was organised in Dublin in May 1897. Listed as being on the platform, alongside Douglas Hyde, John MacNeill (editor the Gaelic Journal) and Rev. M.P. Hickey (Professor of Irish at Maynooth) was M. Lowe, Gaelic League, Liverpool. A special welcome was extended to T.H. Thomas, Herald Bard of the Gorsedd, Wales. It was the Welsh Eisteddfod which provided the inspiration for the Oireachtas.[220] The fact that Michael Lowe was on the platform would indicate that the Liverpool Gaelic League was at the very heart of the revival movement. F. McCollum, of the London Gaelic League was also present, as was J.Rogers from Barrow-in-Furness. Various competitions were organised for the Oireachtas, and the winning essay, written in Irish, under the theme 'The influence of language on nationality' was won by Norma Borthwick, of the London branch.

Norma Borthwick (1862-1934) was to be one of the best-known figures of the revival movement. She was born in Highfield, Higher Bebington, on the Cheshire side of the River Mersey (which now forms part of the county of Merseyside). Her father was listed as 'General merchant' on her birth certificate. He mother was from Edinburgh. She first came to prominence in Ireland during the Land War, when Plan of Campaign activists encouraged English visitors to witness the widespread evictions which were taking place. MPs were amongst those who went to Ireland as observers, and one of these, Charles Conybeare, the 36 year-old Liberal representative for Camborne in Cornwall, was arrested in 1889 and imprisoned for taking part in a criminal conspiracy, namely the Plan of Campaign. The eviction he witnessed took place on the Olphert estate, in the strongly Irish-speaking area of Falcarragh, Co. Donegal. Norma Borthwick, a gifted artist, sketched the events that took place and her work appeared in a special supplement in the United Irishman in October and November 1890. She became active in the Gaelic League in Dublin soon after its formation in 1893. Liam P. O' Riain makes reference to her in The Irish Literary Revival (1894) :"Miss Norma Borthwick who is known as an artist will be remembered by many readers in connection with the exciting episodes in the Land War in Ireland." By 1897 she was in London, where she became one of a number of Merseyside Irish-speakers who played a prominent part in the Gaelic League there. In June 1898 she was appointed secretary of the Gaelic League in Dublin, as well as manager of the Gaelic Journal. She moved to Ireland to take up this role.

To gauge the strength of the language in the city, it is informative to follow the career of Piras Béaslaí (Percy Beasley 1881-1965). He learned Irish at home, where his journalist father used to supply him with copies of The Gaelic Journal. After attending the Oireachtas in Dublin in May 1900, he enrolled at the Gaelic League (GL) classes at Copperas Hill, but was not impressed with the standard.[221] He enrolled at the Bootle branch in 1902 in order to take advantage of the fact that there were a lot of native speakers, mainly from Mayo, connected with the Gaelic League in the north end. It is interesting to note that the organisation attracted people from different classes and sexes and with differing levels of ability in the language. The native speakers appear to have been more than willing to share their language with the second generation and members of the second generation were to make an outstanding contribution to the revival.

Piaras Béaslaí was born in Breckfield Road South, Everton. His mother was from Limerick while his father, P.J. Beasley was from Kerry and was editor of Fr Nugent's Catholic Times newspaper. The area was a prosperous, middle-class district before it was overwhelmed by the expansion of working class housing in the city in the 1890's. Some of the large houses from that era remain, but not the Béaslaí residence. A plaque commemorating the poet was unveiled at the Strawberry Tavern in Breckfield Road South in October 2004 by Professor Pádraig Ó Siadhail, Béaslaí's biographer. The event was organised by the Liverpool GL.

Béaslaí attended St Francis Xavier's College, in Shaw Street, north of the city centre, before it moved to Woolton in 1961. Opened in 1842, the school was :"to be conducted by masters from, and in connection

---

[220] Gaelic Journal June 1897 page 1

[221] O Siadhail Op cit p 51-52

with, Stonyhurst." [222] Situated in north Lancashire, Stoneyhurst is one of the premier Catholic public schools in England, and its ethos was to be imposed on the mainly Irish population of SFX. By 1930, with 13,000 members, this was the largest Catholic parish in the whole country, and the college, with 680 pupils, was the largest Catholic secondary school. Béaslaí wrote of it thus in 1955 :"It makes me melancholy to think of all those boys of pure Irish blood lost to Ireland, educated by the Jesuits into hundred-per-cent Englishmen." [223]

Although he was unimpressed by the first Irish classes he attended in Liverpool, he was to write later :"However, in the long run my work in the Gaelic League was beneficial. It brought me in contact with many good Irish speakers. Most of them were Mayomen, of whom a great many had emigrated to Merseyside, and I enlarged my knowledge of Irish by becoming familiar with the Mayo dialect. I met one Kerryman who was one of the best speakers of Irish I ever met." [224]

Many of these Irish speakers worked together on the docks, where they would have been able to use their mother tongue on a daily basis. The Gaelic League organised regular social events, such as traditional dances (céilithe) and music sessions, where Irish speakers socialised. Such occasions provided an opportunity for learners like Béaslaí to put into practice what they had learnt in class. The increased number of priests with Irish also meant that Irish-speakers had more opportunity to practice their religion through their language. All these factors helped to create viable Irish-speaking communities in Liverpool. We get an indication of this from a letter Béaslaí wrote to his uncle, Jemmie Long, in Clonmel, Co. Waterford, in April 1901. In it he describes attending a hurling match between Liverpool and Manchester, at which he heard nothing but Irish spoken all around him. He said that there were hundreds of speakers of the language in Liverpool. [225]

However, it is also clear that many Irish-speakers turned their backs on the language as they realised that English was the language they and their children required for economic and social advancement in England. Writing around 1876, John Stuart Blackie, Professor of Celtic Studies at Edinburgh University, bemoaned , "The horrible materialism that asks, 'Where will Irish carry you when you cast loose from Dublin quays?', measures everything by money value or mechanical utility, and contemptuously scouts every value but its own." [226] Patrick Pearse came across this attitude in Rosmuc, Co. Galway, around 1888. As he urged the locals to cherish their native language: " ...they listened to him for ten minutes but his speech was brought to an abrupt end when a voice shouted :'Is beag an mhaith í nuair a ghabhann tú thar an Teach Dóite'. " (It is of little use to you when you go beyond the Teach Dóite. (The place that marked the start of the English-speaking area)[227]

As Karen Corrigan says in her essay: "It is evident that the decline in Gaelic during this period was also rooted in the Irish psyche, which had come to perceive the acquisition of English as a prerequisite of social and economic advancement in an expanding and increasingly urbanised world."

Béaslaí would appear to have come across this sort of attitude in Liverpool, for he wrote in 1914 :"Deirtear go bhfuil i bhfad níos mó Gaedhilgeóiribh i Liverpool Shasana ná i mBaile Átha Cliath. Ach níl éin mheas aca ar an nGaedhilg..." [228]"It is said that there are more Irish speakers in Liverpool, England, than there are in Dublin. But they have no respect for the language." He wrote this when there were five branches of the Gaelic League operating under the Liverpool District Committee, of which he was the secretary for a period. It was this committee which invited Patrick Pearse (then editor of the GL newspaper An Claidheamh Soluis) to give a lecture entitled 'The Story of the Gaelic League' in the Picton Library, Liverpool on October 4, 1904.[229] The current GL branch invited Pádraig Ó Siadhail to give a lecture in the same venue on October 4, 2004. The lecture was about the life of Piaras Béaslaí, who had been in the 1904 audience.

---

[222] Whitehead M (ed) Held in Trust. Stonyhurst 2008. P 142

[223] O Siadhai ibid p 17

[224] O Siadhail. op cit p 52

[225] O Siadhail. ibid p 55

[226] Ni Mhuiríosa. op cit p 1

[227] O Cuiv. op cit p 87

[228] O Siadhail op cit p 59

[229] An Claidheamh Soluis October 29 1904

When Béaslaí enrolled in the Bootle GL branch in 1902, he met Alphonsus Ó Labhradha, who, like him, was born in Liverpool and learnt to speak Irish in the city. Like Béaslaí, he produced some outstanding plays in Irish, one of which, An tSnaidhm (The Knot) won the first prize in the drama competition at the Oireachtas in Dublin in 1910. He told his fellow Irish-speakers there that he had previously only spent four days in Ireland in his entire life. He was president of Bootle GL at the time, and the Liverpool branch still possesses an original copy of his play, providing documentary proof that the language was passed down to the second generation. His one-act comedy A West Briton's Romance was also a huge success. Unfortunately for Liverpool, he subsequently emigrated to the USA. A collection of Piaras Béaslaí's poems : Bealtaine 1916 agus Dánta Eile, was republished by Coiscéim in Dublin in 1991.

Irish speakers from other counties, such as Leitrim and Galway, also settled in Bootle, a fact referred to by John Pinkman (1902 – 1970) in his book 'In the Legion of the Vanguard.' In chapter one he writes of his parents. They were born in rural Leitrim in the 1850s and spoke Irish together at home and carried on many traditional customs and practices bound up in the language.

Liverpool is particularly interesting in the way it brought together so many different strands of the Irish language movement- the original famine refugees, the second generation, and the Celtic scholars. Kuno Meyer was in regular contact with Celtic scholars in Ireland, as his letter - from his address at 57 Hope Street, Liverpool - dated March 1896, and published in The Gaelic Journal of May 1896, shows. He delivered a lecture to the Liverpool branch of the Gaelic League on October 26, 1904, not long after his return from a trip to Hungary. He argued that the Irish could learn valuable lessons from the revival of the Hungarian language and literature, adding :"I desire most earnestly to promote the cause of the Gaelic Movement which, from its inception, has had my heartfelt sympathy and, so far as I have been able to give it, my co-operation." [230] In April 1912 Meyer travelled to Dublin where he and Fr Peadar O' Laoghaire were conferred with the Freedom of the City in tribute to their work for the Irish language.

Dr Mark Ryan, who passed through Liverpool as a child in 1860, having being evicted three times with his family, was the driving force behind the foundation of the O'Growney branch of the Gaelic League in London in 1896. On the branch committee was Stiofán Mac Enna, (Stephen McKenna) who was born and raised in Liverpool. Norma Borthwick sang at their concert on Lá Fhéile Bríde, 1897.[231]

Micheal Davitt, who passed through Liverpool as a famine refugee with his family, was one of five members of Parliament who were on the national council of the Gaelic League. In 1906 Davitt wrote, in a letter to The Nationalist, :"My idea of an Irish Ireland is an Ireland as politically independent as we can make it; with all her people well-educated- in Gaelic, and in English, and in as many other languages as they wish to learn...," [232] By this time Davitt had won international respect for his successful work with the Land League. He was the first Irishman to visit Leo Tolstoy (1828-1910) in Russia in June ,1904, when he appealed for his help in the struggle against the British Government. He visited him again in February, 1905, and this time he was accompanied by Liverpool-born GL member Stiofán Mac Enna (Stephen McKenna, 1872-1934), who, like Davitt, was a respected writer and journalist. McEnna interviewed Tolstoy about Bloody Sunday (9 January 1905). His account of his visit was published in The Irish Statesman 1/10/1927. [233] Tolstoy referred to the Irishmen as "lovely, vigorous and merry people." [234] It is interesting to contrast this view with that of the Picturesque Handbook Of Liverpool, and Punch, quoted earlier in this book. MacEnna was working as European correspondent for Joseph Pulitzer's New York World at the time, and was a popular member of the Irish colony in Paris, being friends with the likes of Maud Gonne, JM Synge and James Joyce.

As noted earlier, MacEnna was one of the founder members of the O'Growney branch of the GL in London in October 1896. After his visit to Tolstoy he went on to work on the GL newspaper, An Claidheamh Soluis, with Patrick Pearse in Dublin. He listened to Pearse read the Proclamation at the start of the Rising in 1916 and although he was not in the IRB he offered to help out in the GPO. His offer was rejected on the grounds of his ill health. He was the subject of the book Mo Chara Stiofán (1939) by Liam O Rinn (1886-1943) and even gets a mention in Ulysses : "- Mallarmé, don't you know, he said, has

[230] O Lúing Op cit pp 37-38

[231] O Súilleabháin, D. Conradh na Gaeilge i Londain 1894-1917 p 6

[232] King, C. Michael Davitt UCD 2009. P 4

[233] Journal and Letters of Stephen McKenna. London 1936. www.archive.org

[234] Makovitskii, D. www.bl.uk British Library help for researchers- Tolstoy, visitors.

written those wonderful prose poems Stephen McKenna used to read to me in Paris."[235]

One of the Liverpool-born persons active in the London GL was Sadhbh Trinseach (Cesca Trench, 1891-1918). She was born in the vicarage of St John the Baptist's Church in Tuebrook, about a mile from the birthplace of Piaras Béaslaí. Like him, her parents were Irish. Her father, Herbert Francis Chenevix Trench, was vicar at St John's. In another event organised by the Gaelic League, a plaque in her memory was unveiled at the vicarage by her grand-nephew, Anthony Fletcher, in May 2008. Cesca Trench trained as an artist in Paris and then moved to Dublin in 1914 to join her family. She designed Gaelic Christmas cards and clothes. Some of her sketches appeared in An Claidheamh Soluis 1913-14, as well as a letter in Irish, November 1, 1912. She was great friends with Stephen McKenna and his wife Mary Bray.

Cesca Trench's diary for the turbulent period 1913-1916 formed the basis of the book Cesca's Diary[236] and the Irish TV documentary of the same name. Some of her paintings are in the National Gallery of Ireland. The book Cesca's Diary features a sketch of Piaras Béaslaí, with whom she became friendly in Dublin. He had moved to the Irish capital in 1905, two years after the publication of his first Irish poem. He became immersed in the cultural revival and nationalist politics in Dublin and was a leading figure in the Easter Rising, 1916. Sentenced to penal servitude by a military court, it was while he was incarcerated in England that he produced some of his most outstanding poetry, including Bealtaine 1916. He escaped from prison twice. Elected to the first Dáil Éireann (Irish parliament), he supported the Anglo-Irish Treaty of 1922 and was made a general in the Free State Army during the Civil War. He was a close friend of Michael Collins. He resigned all his official positions in 1923 to devote himself to writing in Irish, producing one novel, several plays and many poems. Béaslaí's plays were a hit at Dublin's Abbey Theatre : "On 12 November, 1923, a triple bill of one-act plays in Irish was performed by the Gaelic Players. These were the acting company of a new formation, An Comhar Drámaíochta, established by Piaras Béalsaí, Gearóid Ó Lochlainn and others to promote drama in Irish, which had been almost entirely neglected by the Abbey since its inception."[237] Two more of Béaslaí' plays were produced at the Abbey the following year : Cluiche Cártaí and Beirt na Bodhaire . The Irish Statesman commented : "Seldom have I enjoyed a heartier bout of uproarious laughter than at the Abbey....when...Cluiche Cartaí was given."[238] The play was produced by Gearóid Ó Lochlainn, who also acted in it.

Like Béaslaí, Ó Lochlainn (Gerard Patrick O' Loughlin, 1884-1970) was born in Liverpool, the only one of a family of six children who was not born in Ireland. The family moved back there when he was a child. He is listed in the 1901 census as living with his father, Patrick and mother Elizabeth, in Tullamore, Co. Offaly. Both men are listed as Irish-speakers. Gearóid Ó Lochlainn had a number of essays and poems published in An Claidheamh Soluis and Fáinne an Lae and began acting in Irish-language plays in Dublin in 1903. He enrolled at Copenhagen University in 1907, where he studied languages, philosophy and psychology. He translated plays by Ibsen (1828-1906) into Irish as well as plays in Danish, German and English.

Clearly, then, the Liverpool-Irish made an outstanding contribution to the Gaelic Revival of the late 19th and early 20th century. These five Irish speakers were influenced by a vigorous Irish speaking culture on Merseyside. Their command of the language and their understanding of its heritage was such that each of them went on to make a substantial contribution to the wider Irish language movement in Britain and Ireland.

THE IRISH LANGUAGE AND THE LIVERPOOL DIALECT

There is evidence that Irish speakers made a major contribution to the local Liverpool dialect , known as Scouse. Numerous words from Irish passed into the local speech , something commented on by visitors like the American journalist John Weis Forney (1817-81) . After visiting St John's Market one Saturday night in 1867, he commented :"Although the surging mass in which I was tossed about spoke my own language, it was very difficult to realize it in the jargon that filled my ears, a patois in which the broad English and the broader Scotch, and the rapid Irish, were strangely commingled." [239]

[235] Joyce, J. Ulysses, Paris 1922. Penguin edition 1969 p 187

[236] Pyle, H. Cesca's Diary 1913-1916. Dublin 2005

[237] Welsh, R. The Abbey Theatre 1899-1999. Oxford 1999

[238] O Siadhail .Op cit. p 632

[239] Seed, D (ed) American Travellers in Liverpool Liverpool UP 2008. P 175

An English writer, around 1900, was more critical. Describing the slums of the north end, "where the majority are either Irish or of Irish descent," Dixon Scott said :"It follows, therefore, that here alone in Liverpool do you get a specific dialect. They speak a bastard brogue : a shambling, degenerate speech of slip shod vowels and muddied consonants- a cast-off clout of a tongue, more debased even than Whitechapel Cockney, because so much more sluggish, so much less positive and acute." [240]

The local people would not have realised that their dialect of English contained numerous Irish words, but clearly it was noticed by people from outside the community. In the 1960s people from the city were termed 'wackers' by outsiders because of their habit of referring to each other by the Irish word 'mhac' (pronounced 'wack' , it is the word for son -mac- with lenition, which is used when addressing someone). Strictly speaking, the vocative case ' a mhic' should be used, but both appear in colloquial speech, sometimes together, as in : 'A mhac! A mhic ó!' [241] The Liverpool comedian Tommy Hanley used the expression on his radio show in the 1940s. Perhaps because outsiders drew attention to it, and mocked it, the word has all but dropped out of the dialect. It crops up in the Christy Moore song : The Crack was 90 in the Isle of Man. Wack also appears in Jim Fitsimon's book A Brief History of St Augustines, Great Howard Street, 1849-1976. He also uses the word 'gansey' which is the Irish word 'geansaí', meaning pullover.

Another Irish word that survives in the north end is 'féasóg' (beard) although now it is often used to mean 'face.' Cac is one Gaelic word that every Scouser would understand. The words 'slapáil' meaning slovenliness and 'slapóg' meaning a sloppy, slovenly woman, seemed to have morphed together into the scouse word 'slapper.' Many Irish speakers recognise the Liverpool farewell ' ta rah' as being a compressed from of 'Tabhair Aire' (take care) which is a common Gaelic farewell and is pronounced 'tooher arer.' The Irish phrase 'is maith sin' meaning 'that's good' has been compressed into the word 'smashin' in Liverpool, which sounds almost the same as the Gaelic and means exactly the same thing. The use of the word 'youse,' being the plural of 'you' (tá sibh as opposed to tá tú in Irish) is typical of Hiberno-English.

Pat O' Mara's autobiography contains much Hiberno-English, which is heavily influenced by Gaelic. He was third generation Irish . Thus we have sentences like 'There came a knock on the door, ' a phrase which – though in English - utilises Gaelic idiom. The dialogue in the book is similarly influenced, for example with the use of the Gaelic diminutive 'ín' (pronounced 'een') :"You wouldn't open the door would you, little maneen, eh?" says his Liverpool-born father. As with Pat Fitsimmons, Irish words are used, but with an Anglicised spelling eg Colleen (cailín), shillelagh (sail éille), banshee (bean sí).

He was clearly familiar with the Gaelic practice of 'ag caoineadh' or 'keening' as watch was kept over a body the night before a funeral :"As the wake proceeded into the night, with the usual Celtic moaning and crying and joking." [242]

CONCLUSION.

In this book I have explored some of the documentary evidence that supports my contention that the Irish language was widely spoken in Liverpool throughout the nineteenth century, and before.

Amongst this evidence is A Petition from the Irish Catholics of Liverpool to Propaganda, signed by 24,000 people in 1842, which requested Rome to provide more Irish-speaking priests for the city as many people there could not attend church services as they could not speak English.

The Irish language abstinence pledge, administered by Fr Mathew the following year, is further evidence of the use of Irish in Liverpool.

Canon Abraham Hume's Survey of 1850 - Missions at Home - provides us with detailed statistical data for the use of the Irish language in the Vauxhall/St Stephen's area during the Famine period (1845-52). In addition we have two autobiographies written by famine refugees of this period: Michael Davitt and Mark Ryan as well as reports from coroners courts concerning famine refugees who were unable to speak English, a fact commented on by Rev Johns in Liverpool in 1847.

[240] Scott, D & Hamilton Hay, J. Liverpool. London 1907

[241] O Dónaill, N. Foclóir Gaeilge-Béarla. Dublin 1977. P 813

[242] O Mara, P. Op cit. P 49

The census figures of 1851 show 80 per cent of the population in many areas of the west of Ireland, where many of the famine refugees to Liverpool originated, were still Irish-speaking, despite the great loss of life and emigration caused by the Famine.

The writings of James Carling and others provide evidence that the language was passed on to the second generation.

In short, the hundreds of thousands of Irish people who arrived in Liverpool brought with them one of the oldest languages and richest cultural heritages in Europe. Unfortunately, the country they arrived in was by and large hostile to them and their culture, with a few noble exceptions, such as the Rev. Abraham Hume, who took it upon himself to learn their beautiful language in Liverpool.

The commemoration of the famine in Liverpool in 1997 demonstrated an awareness of the impact of this event on the Irish language. The Commemoration Committee commissioned a series of plaques, in Irish and English, which were unveiled at places in the city associated with the famine, such as the entrance to Clarence Dock mentioned at the start of this book. The Committee also commissioned the memorial, made by sculptor Eamonn O'Docherty, which stands in St Luke's Gardens and carries the words :Coinnigh Cuimhne ar an Gorta Mór/ Remember the Great Famine.

The committee was determined that the thousands of refugees who perished in the city would be more than "figures in a notebook." [243] When a commemoration service was held in St Anthony's Church, Scotland Road in October 1997 for the 2,303 victims who were buried in an unmarked mass grave there in 1847, all their names appeared in the handbook for the service. Frank Neal spoke of the refugees thus :"Mostly from the Gaelic speaking area of the West, Roscommon, Mayo, Galway and Sligo, they were rural people, disorientated and confused, most never having even experienced sea journeys and life in large towns."[244] Local Irish musicians from Comhaltas Ceoltoirí Éireann played An Ghaoth Aneas (The South Wind) by O' Carolan, which would have delighted James Carling.

Despite all the opposition and hardship, the Irish language endured in Liverpool throughout the nineteenth century, so that the Irish community in the city were to make an outstanding contribution to the cultural revival that occurred as the twentieth century approached.

    Tony Birtill

Críoch

[243] Taylor, AJP. (1906-1990) Genocide . New Statesman 23/11/62 .

[244] The Great Hunger Commemoration Service. St Anthony's. 3/10/1997

Bibliography

1. Unpublished sources and manuscripts

National Library of Ireland :

MS 10,972. Letters and papers of Pádraig Ciosóg, treasurer of Liverpool Gaelic League 1915-1922.

MS 8435-8436 : Art O Briain Papers

MS 5835 Minutes of Executive meeting INL London.

Liverpool Gaelic League :

Letters of Cáitlín Nic Cába

Notes on the history of the Liverpool Gaelic League. Brian Murphy 1938 (unpublished)

Letters of James Carling (1857-1887) from Michael Kelly, Liverpool.

Gaelic League Headquarters, Dublin : Branch registration books 1893 onwards.

Liverpool Metropolitan Cathedral Archive
S1 II A/1 Early Bishops collection : Bishop Brown papers:
13/1/1847 Circular - collection for the Irish famine.
27/2/1847 Draft against Irish procession in Liverpool

St Anthony's Parish Box Bundle 31
Jubilee of the Church (50th anniversary of opening) brochure
Rededication mass 29/9/1993 - list of priests who have served at St Anthony's 1804- 1989
Found Worthy - Biographical Dictionary of the Secular Clergy of the Archdiocese of Liverpool (deceased)
1850-2000. Brian Plumb (NW Catholic History Society) 2005
Arundel to Zabi- A Biographical Dictionary of the Catholic Bishops of England and Wales (deceased)
1623-1987. Brian Plumb. St Joseph's College, Up Holland.

St Joseph's parish box
St Patrick's parish box including list of priests who served the parish.
St Bridget's parish box

Propaganda Archives (Rome) from Dr Peter Doyle (translated by him from French and Italian). Copyright
Peter Doyle.
APF Scrititure Rif. Anglia Vol 10 pp 225 : A petition from the Irish Catholics of Liverpool to Propaganda
1842.
P. 228 & 268 letters from Edmund Griffin, Liverpool regarding the petition. 1842
Pp 248 & 250 Letters from Bishop Brown.
Pp 256 Propaganda's reply to Griffin. 1843

St Nicholas Church of England, Blundell Sands, Merseyside. Marriage Register and parish records.

All Hallows College, Dublin. Matricula

Unitarian Church Headquarters, London. Transactions of the Unitarian Historical Society

The Irish College, Rome. Papers of Paul Cullen .

Capuchin Archives : Fr Theobald Mathew Collection

University of Liverpool, Special Collections :
Missions at Home . Abraham Hume 1850.
Liverpool Domestic Mission Annual Report (1847) Johns, J.

Liverpool Record Office .
Abraham Hume : Condition of Liverpool 1858
Abraham Hume : Visiting List of the Parish of Vauxhall
Census 1881, 1891, 1901.
Gores Directory 1839-1841. 1873
283 PET 2/51 Baptism Register for St Peters. 4/9/1861 . Entry 166
The Liverpool Irish Herald. No.1. Saturday October 31 1885

Public Record Office of Northern Ireland :

Abraham Hume papers D 27656

Northern Ireland Assembly Record

Bootle Library (Orrell Branch) :

Henders, S, ' The Shamrock and the Lily : Sectarianism in 'Brutal' Bootle 1868-1914 ' unpublished MA
thesis 1989-190

Ormskirk Library :
Bradshaw, PE : A Study of the Township of Ormskirk in the mid-nineteenth Century based on the Royal
Report of the Population Census 1851. 1979

Contemporary Newspapers/periodicals

The Chester Chronicle Jan 1846- Nov 1847
The Catholic Times
The Catholic Herald

Irisleabhar na Gaeilge /The Gaelic Journal 1882 onwards

Fáinne an Lae 1898 onwards

An Claidheamh Soluis 1899 onwards

The Liverpool Echo. The Daily Post.
The Times

Contemporary Books/publications

The Dublin Magazine Volume 1 (e book)
Il Piccolo della Sera (Trieste) 16/9/1907
Béaslaí. P. An Sgaothaire agus Cúig Drámaí Eile.Dublin 1929
Béaslaí. P. Bealtaine 1916 agus Danta Eile. 1920 (New edition 1991)
Brooke, R. Liverpool as it Was 1775-1800. New edition Liverpool 2003
Burke, Thomas. Catholic History of Liverpool. Liverpool 1910
Carleton, William. Traits and Stories of the Irish Peasantry. (2 vols) 1830
Campbell, J & Campbell-Hardcastle, MS. Lives of Lord Lyndhurst & Lord Broughton. London 1869
Connolly, James. Labour in Irish History 1910.
Cork Historical and Archaelogical Society, Journal of. Volume 1. 1892
Davis, Thomas. Prose Writings: Essays on Ireland. Walter Scott Publishing, London 1908
Davitt : The Fall of Feudalism in Ireland(Harper ,London 1904)

66

Denvir, John : Life Story of an Old Irish Rebel. 1910
        The Irish in Britain. 1894
Engels, Frederick. The Condition of the Working Class in England in 1844. (Panther 1976)
Finch, J. Statistics of the Vauxhall Ward, 1842. Facsimile edition Liverpool 1986.
Hyde, Douglas : The Necessity for De-Anglicising Ireland, in The Revival of Irish Literature; Charles Gavan Duffy (ed) 1894.
Joyce, James. Ulysses. 1922. Penguin edition 1977
Joyce, James. Dubliners (1914) Alan Sutton edition 1992
Mitchel, J. Jail Journal 1854. Gill, Dublin 1921
        The Last Conquest of Ireland
O'Labhraidh, A. An tSnaidhm. Dublin 1910.
O'Labhraidh, A. A West Briton's Romance. Bootle 1907
O'Leary, Peadar. Mo Scéal Féin. Brún agus O Nualláin 1915
O'Leary, Peter. My Story (translation by Cyril T. O Céirin). Mercier Press 1970
O'Mara, P. Autobiography of a Liverpool-Irish Slummy. 1933
Smiles, Samuel. History of Ireland under the Government of England. London 1844
Trevelyan, Charles. The Irish Crisis. London 1848

Secondary Sources. Irish
Feasta (magazine) March 2008
Birtill. T. Articles on www.beo.ie May 2001 onwards. Including editions 15,23,32,35, 55, 80, 93,94,98,104, 114
Denvir, G (eag) Duanaire an Chéid . Cló Iar-Chonnachta, Conamara 2000
Denvir, G & Ní Dhonnchadha, A. Gearrscéalta an Chéid. Cló Iar-Chonnachta. 2000
Mac Aonghusa, P. Ar Son na Gaeilge: Conradh na Gaeilge 1893-1993. Dublin 1993.
Ní Mhuiriosa, M. RéamhChonaitheoirí. Dublin 1978
O'Brien, F. An Piarsach Óg agus Conradh na Gaeilge. Dublin 1969
O Fiannachta, P. An Biobla Naofa. An Sagart, Maigh Nuad 1981
Ó Glaisne, R. Dúbhglas de h-Íde 1860-1949. Dublin 1991
        De bhunadh Protastúnach. Carbad 2000
Ó Siadhail, P. An Béaslaíoch. Beatha agus Saothar Phiaras Béaslaí 1881-1965. Dublin 2007.
Gearrdhrámaí an Chéid . Cló Iar-Chonnachta, Conamara. 2000.

Ó Súilleabhán, D. Conradh na Gaeilge i Londain 1894-1917.
        An Piarsach agus Conradh na Gaeilge. Dublin 1980
        Na Timirí 1893-1927.   Dublin 1990.
OTuama, S agus Kinsella, T. An Duanaire 1600-1900. Dublin 1981.
Póirtéir, C. Gnéithe An Ghorta. Dublin 1995
Watson, S (ed) Oideas Gael, 25 Bliain faoi Bhláth. Donegal 2007

Secondary Sources. English

Ascott, Lewis & Power. Liverpool 1660-1750. Liverpool UP 2006
Beck, G. The English Catholics 1850-1950. London 1950
Belcham, J. Irish, Catholic and Scouse. Liverpool UP 2007
Berresford Ellis, P. James Connolly Selected Writings. London 1973
        A History of the Irish Working Class. London 1985
Boyne, P. John O'Donovan (1806-1861). Boethius, Kilkenny. 1987
Cahill, Corish, PJ. Maynooth T How the Irish Saved Civilization Hodder and Stoughton 1995
Cashmore, Ellis. Dictionary of Race and Race Relations.
Catholic Life (May 2013)- article on Luigi Gentili by Foley D.A. The Universe Media Group.
Cheshire Local History Association. Cheshire History no. 51 2011-12
Connolly, SJ. Oxford Companion to Irish History. OUP 1998.
College 1795-1995. Dublin 1995
Corkery, D. The Fortunes of the Irish Language. Cork 1954
Curtis, L. Nothing but the Same Old Story. London 1984
        The Cause of Ireland. Belfast 1994
De Blácam, A. Gaelic Literature Surveyed. Talbot Press, Dublin.

Doherty & Hickey A Chronology of Irish History since 1500. Dublin 1989
Doyle, P. Mitres and Missions in Lancashire. The RC Diocese of Liverpool 1850-2000. Liverpool Bluecoat 2005
Dudley Edwards, R. An Atlas of Irish History. Methuen, London 1973
Duffy, S (ed) Atlas of Irish History. Dublin 1997.
Dunleavy J&W. Douglas Hyde. University of California Press. 1991.
Elliot, M. The Catholics of Ulster. London 2001
Fitzsimons, J. St Augustines, Gt Howard St. A Brief History 1849-1976. Liverpool 1997
Foley, DA. Fr Luigi Gentili in Catholic Life May 2013
Furnival, J. Children of the Second Spring (Fr Nugent). Gracewing, Hereforshire 2006
George Boyce, D. Nineteenth Century Ireland. Gill & MacMillan. 2005
Gillespie, W. The Christian Brothers in England 1825-1880. Burleigh Press Bristol 1975
Grant, R.G. The Holocaust. Hodder/Wayland. 1998
Harrison-Therman, D. Stories from Tory Island. Dublin 1983
Hayden, A. Footprints of Father Mathew. Dublin 1947
Higham, D. Liverpool and the '45 Rebellion .Countryvise 1995
Hollet, D. Passage to the New World. Heaton, Gwent 1995
Holt, RV. The Unitarian Contribution to Social Progress in England. London 1952
Ihde, TW.The Irish Language in the United States.
Kee, R. Ireland a History. London 1980
Kelly, M. Liverpool, The Irish Connection. Liverpool 2003.
Kineally, C. This Great Calamity : Irish Famine 1845-52. Gill & McMillan, Dublin 1994
The famine 1845-52. How England Failed Ireland. Modern History Review. Sept 1995
Beyond Revisionism : reassessing the famine. History Ireland winter 1995
Food Exports from Ireland 1846-47. History Ireland Spring 1997
Lees, Lynn Hollen . Exiles of Erin: Irish Migrants in Victorian London. Manchester U.P 1979
MacDonagh, O. O'Connell 1775-1847. London 1991
Mac Réamoinn (ed) The Pleasures of Gaelic Poetry. Allen Lane, London 1982
Mangan, J (ed) Robin Wyte's 1847 Famine Ship Diary. Mercier 1994
Moffit, M. The Society for Irish Church Missions to the Roman Catholics, 1849-1950. Manchester UP 2005
Moody, TW & Martin FX (eds) The Course of Irish History. NY 1967
Morris, JM. Into the Crucible (Widnes). Birkenhead 2005.
Mistéil, P (ed) The Irish Language and the Unionist Tradition. Ultach Trust 1994
Murray, D. The Holy Cross Church Centenary 1849-1948. Pub: Fr Murphy, Holy Cross, Liverpool 1948
Neal, F. Sectarian Violence, The Liverpool Experience 1819-1914. MUP 1988
    Black '47. Britain and the Famine Irish Newsham Press Liverpool 2003.
O'Buachalla, B. The Irish Language and the Unionist Tradition. Belfast 1994.
O' Donnell, R. The Irish Famine. O'Brien Press, Dublin 2008
O'Fiannai, S. The Gaelic League in Scotland 1895-1995. Glasgow 1995
O'Fearaíl, P. The Story of Conradh na Gaeilge. Dublin 1975
O'Lúing, S. Kuno Meyer 1858-1919. Dublin 1991.
O'Sullivan, P (ed) The Irish in New Communities. Leicester University Press 1992
O'Tuama ,S (ed) The Gaelic League Idea (Thomas Davis Lectures) Cork 1972
O'Tuathaigh, G. Ireland Before the Famine 1798-1840. Dublin 2007.
Pinkman J . In the Legion of the Vanguard. Mercier Press. 1998
Póirtéir, C (ed) The Great Irish Famine. RTE/Mercier 1995
Runaghan, P. Fr Nugent's Liverpool 1849-1905. Birkenhead 2003
Ryan, M. Fenian Memories. Dublin 1945
Seed, D (ed) American Travellers in Liverpool. LUP 2008
Smith, D. The Holocaust : A Guide for Police Personnel. The Holocaust Centre, Notts. 2008.
Swift, R & Gilley, S. The Irish in Britain 1815-1939. London 1989
Taylor, AJP. Essays in Nineteenth Century Europe. Faber & Faber London 2008
Thompson, EP. The Making of the English Working Class. Pelican London 1968
Ultach Trusr/Foras na Gaeilge . An Ghaeilge. Belfast 2012

APPENDICES

Appendix One : Use of the term 'extermination'.

In chapter one I use the word 'extermination' to describe what happened to the million plus Irish people who died during the famine 1845-1852. I use this word because it was used by the people involved at the time : both victims and government officials. For example, the poet Brian O Luanaigh, who wrote of "the odious extermination of ' 47."[245]

Lord Lucan, who evicted thousands of Irish-speaking peasants from his huge estates in County Mayo , including five-year-old Michael Davitt who passed through Liverpool with his family en-route to Haslingden, was called 'the old exterminator' by his victims. Michael Davitt described the period thus : : "That eviction and the privations of the preceding famine years, the story of the starving peasants of Mayo, of the deaths from hunger, and the coffinless graves on the roadside-everywhere a hole could be dug for the slaves who died because of 'God's Providence, - all this was the political food, seasoned with a mother's fears over unmerited sorrows and sufferings, which had fed my mind in another land, a teaching which lost none of its force or directness by being imparted in the Gaelic tongue, which was almost always spoken in our Lancashire home." [246]

Póirtéir points out that the famine created more devastation in the Gaelic-speaking West and South West than it did in the rest of the country :"D'fhág seo rian láidir ar thráidisiún béil na ndaoine go ginearálta agus ar thraidisiúin na Gaeltachta go speisialta," - This left a strong impression on the oral tradition of the people generally, and especially on the tradition in the Gaeltacht."[247]

The Irish Folklore Commission collected a huge amount of oral history from ordinary people in the 1930s and 1940s and as Máirin Nic Eoin[248] points out, although only 25% of the people who supplied information about the famine were Gaelic speakers, 40% of the material that was collected on the subject was in that language, illustrating the disproportionate affect the famine had on that section of the community. Furthermore, Comac O Gráda points out that the quality of the information collected on the subject of the famine in Irish was far richer than that collected in English.[249] Unfortunately, as some modern-day academics cannot speak or read Irish, the testimony of the ordinary people passes them by and they are left to formulate their own version of history, often from an entirely Anglo-centric perspective.

There are numerous contemporary references in English to the extermination. The landlord Major Denis Mahon evicted thousands of tenants from his estate in Roscommon and had them packed aboard ships like the Virginius and Erin's Hope which sailed from Liverpool in summer 1847, bound for Canada. [250]. Most of them died en route, or at the Grosse Isle quarantine station at Quebec. Mahon chose the Liverpool route as it was cheapest. When news of the deaths reached Ireland, the Bishop of Elphin wrote an article for the Freeman's Journal, headlined : "Extermination by Thousands !. The Strokestown Massacre Developed."[251]
The Bishop held Denis Mahon accountable for the deaths of 3,006 men, women and children and he listed every one of their names.
"Major Mahon willed the annihilation, the law confirmed it, and the 28 townlands were reduced to solitude and three thousand....driven forth in misery and mourning..."

Denis Mahon was assassinated before this article was written.

[245] Pórtéir, C. Gnéithe an Ghorta. Dublin 1995 p 98

[246] Davitt, M. Fall of Feudalism in Ireland, ch. Xvii.

[247] Póirtéir Ibid p 131

[248] Póirtéir Ibid p 107

[249] Póirtéir Ibid. p. 108

[250] Hollett, D. Passage to the New World. Gwent 1995. Pp 176-177

[251] Laxton, E. The Famine Ships. London 1996. p 73

The Davitt family weren't the only famine refugees who regarded what was happening as an extermination. Speaking at a meeting in Liverpool in 1851, the Irish priest, Rev. Dr Cahill , described what was happening to "our race" as " social and political annihilation."[252]

John Denvir (1834-1916) wrote :"Young as I was, I shall never forget the days of the Famine, for Liverpool, more than any other place outside of Ireland itself, felt its appalling effects."[253] Later, on the same page, he bemoans the media :"The 'Times' actually gloated over what appeared to be the impending extinction of our race." This may have been a reference to an editorial in The Times in 1865 which stated :"A Catholic Celt will soon be as rare on the banks of the Shannon as a Red Indian on the shores of Manhattan."[254]

Clearly the evictions and deaths continued throughout the century, especially during the Land War. Speaking in Bootle in November, 1887, David Crilly, MP for County Mayo, talked passionately of Ireland as "the land of evictions and extermination, all as a result of English and Tory misrule."[255]

John Mitchel (1815-1875), the son of a Presbyterian clergyman, who himself ran a law practice in Banbridge, Co. Down, travelled to Galway in 1847 to witness the famine first-hand, and was horrified by what he saw. He too referred to it as "the extermination".[256] In articles in the United Irishman newspaper he urged the people to tear up the roads and railways to prevent the huge exports of food which were taking place while thousands starved. The government passed the Treason-Felony Act in April 1848 to stifle such opposition and this was used to try and convict Mitchel in May of that year. He was sentenced to 14 years transportation to Australia, and commenced to write his Jail Journal. In his book The Last conquest of Ireland (perhaps) published in 1861, he stated :"The Almighty, indeed, sent the potato blight, but the English created the Famine." This was a reference to British government policy of the time, a policy carried out by Charles Trevelyan (1807-1886) who was Permanent Secretary to the Treasury 1840-1859.

Edward Twistleton, Chief Commissioner of the Irish Poor Law, was appalled by Westminster's behaviour and when he resigned in protest in March, 1849, he condemned the "indifference of the House of Commons" in pursuing "a policy that must be one of extermination."[257]

When the famine memorial was unveiled in Liverpool in 1997, Prime Minister Tony Blair issued a statement of support which said :"That one million people should have died in what was then part of the richest and most powerful nation in the world is something that still causes pain as we reflect on it today."

As the Davitt family and the thousands of other famine refugees walked across Ireland to catch the boat to Liverpool, burying their dead along the way, they could see the fields of wheat, oats, vegetables and animals, and food convoys, often under military escort, heading towards the ports. As they queued at the dockside, they could see the exports of food being loaded aboard ships. The statistics for the vast amounts of food produced in the country were listed in Thom's Irish Almanac, which was published annually from 1844.

Christine Kinealy[258] in her article 'Food Exports from Ireland' 1846-47' states :"It is generally accepted that by the 1840s, Ireland had become the granary of Britain, supplying the grain-hungry British market sufficient to feed two million people annually. " That is to say, Ireland exported more than enough food to feed those who starved to death or were forced to emigrate. Much of this food came through the Port of Liverpool. For example, in the first nine months of 1847, 75 ships sailed here from just one town, Tralee in

[252] Burke. T. Catholic History of Liverpool. 1910. P 110

[253] Denvir, J. Life Story p 53

[254] Curtis, L . Nothing but the Same Old Story 1984 p 58

[255] Henders, S. Shamrock and the Lily, Sectarianism in 'Brutal' Bootle 1868-1914. MA thesis .

[256] Mitchel, J. Jail Journal xxxviii

[257] O Donnell, R. The Irish Famine, Dublin 2008. P 112

[258] Kinealy, C. History Ireland, Spring, 1997.

Kerry. Kinealy goes into some detail about the many other types of food exported from Ireland during The Great Hunger, including potatoes, exports of which actually increased in 1845, the start of the "famine."

As "part of the richest and most powerful nation in the world" assistance could easily have been provided to Ireland to prevent any loss of life during the period 1845-52. Banning exports of food, as was done in other countries, such as Belgium, which were hit by the potato blight, would have been an obvious starting point. The soup kitchens which the government ran successfully for several months in 1847 showed that Westminster had the resources and planning capability to meet the needs of the starving in Ireland, but Trevelyan ordered their closure in the October of that year. "At its peak, in July 1847, over three million people were receiving free soup rations."[259]

Kinealy estimates that over the seven year period of the famine the British government spent approximately £9.9 million on various relief schemes, which represented only about 0.2 per cent of the British GDP. "Less than ten years later, in the course of the Crimean War (over a three year period) the British government spent £69 million on military expenditure."[260]

Similarly, she points out that the contribution of the British government was far less than the £22 million which had been given 12 years earlier to compensate slave owners in the West Indies for the loss of their slaves, something which was pointed out at the time.[261]

When the historian Cecil Woodham-Smith published her book The Great Hunger in 1962, the English historian AJP Taylor (1906-1990) wrote a review of it entitled 'Genocide'[262] in which he compared what had happened in Ireland to the Nazi extermination camp at Belsen. Following the Nuremberg Trials (1945-47) at which some Nazis claimed to have merely been obeying government instructions, the United Nations drafted the Convention on Genocide, article C) of which states :"Deliberately inflicting on the group conditions of life calculated to bring about its physical destruction in whole or in part;"[263] Taylor clearly felt that this applied to British government policy in Ireland 1845-52.

Trevelyan decided that the famine was over in October 1847, closed the soup kitchens, and wrote a book about the affair .[264] He thought the famine, with its huge loss of life, was a good thing, and states on page one :"Unless we are much deceived, posterity will trace up to that famine the commencement of a salutary revolution in the habits of a nation long singularly unfortunate, and will acknowledge that on this, as on so many occasions, Supreme Wisdom had educed permanent good out of transient evil."

Trevelyan only visited Ireland once during the crisis, in October 1847, but did not leave Dublin. Unlike John Mitchel, he did not travel to Galway to witness the carnage at first hand, because he apparently did not wish to have his judgement clouded by exposure to emotive distraction[265] This reminded me of Joseph Goebbels diary entry with regard to the Holocaust in March, 1942 : "One cannot afford sentimentality in a situation such as this."[266] Goebels committed suicide with his family in 1945. Charles Trevelyan was knighted by Queen Victoria in 1848 and elevated to the House of Lords in 1874.

[259] Kinealy, C. The Famine. Modern History Review. September 1995.

[260] Kinealy, C. Beyond Revisionism- reassessing the Great Irish Famine. History Ireland Winter 1995.

[261] Kinealy, C. Letter published in The Irish Post 21/6/1997.

[262] Taylor, A. New Statesman 23/11/1962). Reprinted in Essays in 19th Century History

[263] Cashmore, E (ed) Dictionary of Race and Ethnic Relations, Routledge 1996

[264] Trevelyan, C. The Irish Crisis in 1848, Longman, London, 1848, reprinted from The Edinburgh Review, January 1848. Available on-line via sss.archive.org

[265] O'Donnell, R. The Irish Famine. Dublin 2008.

[266] Quoted in Grant, RG : The Holocaust. Hodder, London, 2000

Appendix Two :

Táimse im chodladh

Tráthnóinín déanach i gcéin cois leasa dhom
Táimse im chodladh na dúistear mé ;
'Sea dhearcas lem thaobh an spéirbhean mhaisiúil,
Táimse im chodladh ná dúisitear mé;

Ba bhachallach péarlach dréimreach barrachas,
A carnfholt craobhach ag teacht léi ar bhaillecrith,
Is í ag caitheamh na saighead trim thaobh do chealg mé
Táimse im chodladh ná dúistear mé;

Is mo bhuachailín óg a tógadh go ceannasach,
Táimse im chodladh ná dúistear mé;
Do cuiread le fóirneart anonn thar farraige
Táimse im chodladh ná dúistear mé;

Go bhfeicead an lá go mbeidh ár ar Shasanaigh,
Ughaim ar a ndrom 's iad ag treabhadh 's ag branar dúinn
Gan mise bheith ann muna dheannam an maide leo
Táimse im chodladh ná dúisiteat mé.

This is an Aisling or vision poem/song, typical of 18th century Ireland. The man is awoken from his sleep by a beautiful woman (Ireland) and urged to take revenge upon the English.

Appendix Three:

Extract from : Redburn. A novel by Herman Melville (1819-91).

Melville arrived in Liverpool in July 1839 and returned to America the following September. He wrote Redburn 10 years later. Here is an extract.

Chapter 40: Brunswick Dock.

Brunswick Dock, to the west of Prince's, is one of the most interesting to be seen. Here lie the various black steamers (so unlike the American boats, since they have to navigate the boisterous Narrow Seas) plying to all parts of the three kingdoms.
Here you see vast quantities of produce, imported from starving Ireland; here you see the decks turned into pens for oxen and sheep; and often, side by side with these enclosures, Irish deck-passengers, thick as they can stand, seemingly penned in just like the cattle. It was the beginning of July when the Highlander arrived in port; and the Irish labourers were daily coming over by thousands, to help harvest the English crops.

One morning, going into the town, I heard a tramp, as of a drove of buffaloes, behind me; and turning around, beheld the entire middle of the street filled by a great crowd of these men, who had just emerged from Brunswick Dock gates, arrayed in long-tailed coats of hoddin-gray (course, undyed material), corduroy knee-breeches, and shod with shoes that raised a mighty dust. Flourishing their Donnybrook shillelaghs (cudgels), they looked like an irruption of barbarians. They were marching straight out of town into the country; and perhaps out of consideration for the finances of the corporation, took the middle of the street, to save the side-walks.

Reproduced in American Travellers in Liverpool. David Seed, editor. Liverpool University Press 2008.